Hi,
I'm the Ugly Friend

And Other Tales of Not Living Up to My Potential

Greg Howard Jr

To my family, who have always been my biggest supporters and will probably never speak to me again.

The last 'butch' thing I ever did.

"Praise" for *Hi, I'm the Ugly Friend*

None of these things were actually said about this book... Probably.

"That never happened." – My Best Friend

"You're an idiot."   My Brother

"Do you even know Gianni Versace?"   Naomi Campbell

"Is that how you really feel?"   My Mother

"I can't read yet."   My Cousin s Daughter

"Sir, are you working on personal projects on company time?"
My Boss

"We were rooting for you! We were all rooting for you! How dare you!"   Tyra Banks

"What is wrong with you?"   My Father

"You've been served."   Taylor Swift s lawyers

"He had such potential."   My Sixth Grade Teacher

Full Disclosure

Dear Reader,

First and foremost, thank you buying this book. It means the world to me that you saw my half-assed attempt at cover art and thought there may be some merit to what I have to say. I m sorry that you are more than likely going to be disappointed.

If you bought this book because you know me, some of what you read here may or may not be about you. So congratulations? You ve made it, kid? I don t know. I m sorry if I screw up the details or have made myself out to be the hero when in reality I was the one who drooled all over that one drag queen from Vegas.

If you bought this book because we are related, I am so sorry. What follows is not going to be pretty and you will more than likely be disappointed in my life choices. We don t even have to talk about it at holidays. We can all just pretend that you didn t read about the time that I got railed by a YouTube personality who was coked out of their minds and dropped me off at the wrong address the next morning forcing me to walk six blocks in broken flip flops. More on this story later for those that are still with me.

What you are going to read in the following pages is mostly my recollection of my life and some things that I think are funny, also some really embarrassing childhood photos. Did they actually happen the way I remember? Probably not, but like most anecdotes they are usually not 100% true. But, hey, it ll make for a good read and you can always fact check my Facebook later.

I ve been writing this book in my head for almost ten years. Mostly just dog earing moments in my life with a thought of If I ever write a book, that s totally going in it. Well, now I am actually writing a book and I can t recall a single one of those dog eared moments. I m starting to wish I had kept a dream journal, but really I don t hate myself enough for that. I m kidding I hate myself more than that. Nothing against people who keep dream journals, but it s really not for me. I tried it once. Here s an excerpt from one that I had to dig through a box to find:

Barbra Streisand hates you, probably. She says you don't wear sensible enough shoes.

You became a millionaire by cornering the market on Rex Manning Day party planning.

My dreams are weird and disjointed, not unlike any movie that Maggie Gyllenhaal has ever appeared in. I m not entirely familiar with the filmography of Maggie Gyllenhaal.

The reality of this stemmed from constantly hearing from people who know me saying that I was clever, witty, funny, and should totally write a book. Y all are totally going to regret ever saying things like that to me.

By this point I hope you aren t hoping for a big payoff somewhere in what follows because a lot of what you are going to read is just like what you ve just read. Weird, disjointed, kind of dark, and a little rambly. Rambly is a word I just made up. It perfectly describes my writing and conversation style.

An unhealthy amount of coffee and cigarettes were consumed during the creation of this book so I d like to give a shout out to my unofficial sponsors: Folgers Coffee   and Pall Mall   cigarettes. Y all are the true MVPs of my creative process.

If you haven t decided that purchasing this book was a mistake; make yourself a proper cup of tea, settle in, and join me on the adventure that is my terribly awkward life. A proper cup of tea contains both milk and sugar. Otherwise you are just drinking dirty leaf water.

PS. If you are any of the famous people I mention in this please don't sue me for libel. If you are a famous person reading this please mention me in your next interview.

PPS. If you are Zayn Malik please marry me.

I'm the reason we can't have nice things.

Things I Should Have Done Before Writing This Book

01 August 2017: Day One

So this is me, writing a book. Of all the roads I thought I would travel in my life, this was certainly not one that I had ever seriously thought about. But here we are!

Prepare for the shock of your lives when I tell you that I am a lazy writer. Me being lazy is going to be a recurring theme in this book so don t be surprised when it comes up again.

I knew that writing a book was hard, like if it was easy everyone would do it. I figured that I ve got an interesting point of view on life in general so it would be at least an easier uphill battle. I ve got a computer, I ve got something to say let s write a book. At least that s what I thought.

It occurs to me now that maybe there are somethings I might have needed to experience before I sat down to do this or at least before I went ahead and made the book available for pre-sale.

I Have Never been to a Disney Park
We weren t poor growing up, but we certainly weren t flushed with cash. A family vacation of that magnitude would have surely had us eating out of trash cans for a few years. So now here I sit a thirty-something Disney virgin. I could go now if I wanted to. I ve got a good job and some money, but I hate kids and the idea of going to Disney World just no longer holds the appeal that it used to.

Put a sex tape on Tumblr
I talk about sex a lot in this book. Like a lot. I feel like now I have to prove that I m having all the sex in the world. I ve got a couple sexy time videos somewhere; maybe I should put them on Tumblr.

Taken Better Care of My Body
I m a caffeine junkie. I go to work with no less than three energy drinks at a time. I start my day with at least two cups of coffee. Unless my heartrate is the same as that of a hummingbird and I can see through walls; I am basically useless. I can t even write this book without some form of caffeinated beverage to get me going. Caffeine is terrible and I should try to cut it out. Might improve my focus and keep me from making Spotify playlists for every mood I experience in a twenty minute period.

I bet a lot of you thought I was going to mention working out and quitting smoking, didn t you? Ha ha! Joke s on you, kid, even with low self-esteem I don t hate myself that much. My body isn t a temple it s a fun house full of wacky mirrors and bats. Lots of bats.

Not Googled "Average Length of a First Novel"
Just out of curiosity I wanted to know what most people considered a good length for a book. Turns out most of them say a good first novel should be between one and two hundred thousand words. Fuck those people. I m only twenty-two thousand in and I have to fill space with bullshit lists that nobody really cares about. Of course, if I hadn t done that my first endeavor into the writing world would have only been like five pages long and would have exclusively featured transcripts of my favorite drag race audition tapes.

Napped Less
Hahahahahahahaha! Just kidding. Naps are the best.

Joined the DAR
Actually this isn t really something I should have done, *Gilmore Girls* is playing in the background and we re up to the season where Rory drops out of school, moves in with her grandparents and joins the DAR. It s doesn t look all that glamorous.

Watched Less Gilmore Girls
This is legit because let s be honest here: Rory is the absolute worst. Lorelai really should have spent less time trying to be her daughter s bestie and spent more time trying to bang Luke! Amiright? While

we re on the subject, while I don t feel like Rory deserved any of the guys she dated on the show, I feel like Logan was the best fit. Also, she s a bitch for not accepting his marriage proposal in the original show, but then hooks up with him while s he s got a fiancé in the reboot. Sorry for the spoilers if you haven t watched the Netflix reboot yet. But it s like a year old at this point so you should probably get on that.

Will someone read this book and decide it will make an inspiring movie that could possibly star Reese Witherspoon or, god forbid, Julia Roberts? I hope the fuck not! That s not the point in my writing this. I m writing this because I ve got things to say that I feel like people should pay money to read instead of getting stunted version from Facebook.

I m off to Google Disney vacations for lonely gays. See you soon.

Home Movies

Why do I look like Magnum PI? Is Tom Selleck my real father?

In West Philadelphia, born and raised...

No, wait, that s not my story.

I remember it all very well, looking back, it was the summer...

Nope!

In the criminal justice system, the people are represented by two separate...

Oh no, it s not that kind of book

It was the best of times. It was the worst of times...

Fuck! That s not it either. I ll get it right this time, I swear.

Picture it, August 24, 1983. *Return of the Jedi* and *Yentl* are dominating the box office. Yentl wasn t released until December 1983, but it still dominated the box office. I think. The Police (with pre-tantric sex Sting) are all over the radio with that one creepy stalker song. Sally Ride is the first American woman in space that year.

And two kids from Alabama have their first child. Me.

My dad was in the Army. They were stationed in the Great White North. Where the sun doesn t set for like 75 days and then completely disappears for the rest of the year. Is this global warming? Probably not; unless you re of the conservative mindset and then it s punishment for touching yourself at night.

For reference, when you Google the city I was born in there are only four particular points of interest that come up. An arts and cultures museum for those who clearly can t see firsthand by walking down the street how white people stole the land from the indigenous people. An ice museum that offers laser light shows and ice sculptures because why the fuck not? Right? An antique car museum that houses 70 classic cars and offers guided tours. Yes, I would very much like a guided tour of the one room that holds the cars in case I can t figure out how to navigate my way out of the backseat of a Model T. I know fuck all about cars, does a Model T even have a backseat or am I just a tramp and that s the first place my mind goes? And finally, a petting zoo. There s no other description for it. It just says Petting Zoo. It has two five star reviews, so I guess those two people really enjoy petting grizzly bears and caribou. I don t know.

Also, this was a time before there were nine million television channels so there was not a whole lot to do except baby making. I assume. Since we left there I haven t really been privy to a lot of snowy seasons, so I don t know how people act when there s white stuff all around. Unless that white stuff comes in a tiny Ziploc bag and then it s just a typical Saturday night in my late twenties.

I was not, however, conceived in the Mayberry of the Arctic. I m not really sure how or where it went down. I like to tell people I was conceived in the bed of Chevy pickup truck outside of a Hank Williams, Jr. concert. Is that true? Probably not, but it gives people an insight into why I am the way I am. This little side note comes back to bite me in the ass later in life, so just keep that in mind as you continue reading.

Anyway, back to the events leading up to my birth.

Three days before I was actually born, my mom went into false labor. For those who don t know false labor is basically the body s way of prepping for the act of squeezing a watermelon through a button hole. It s completely normal. My parents went to the hospital; the doctor told my parents it wasn t time yet.

The doctor then tells my father that he should take my mom home, put her in a warm bath, give her a six-pack of beer and call him if anything happens. This is completely true. Ask either of my parents and they ll tell you. This was cutting edge 1980s medicine. Give the pregnant lady a sixer and see what shakes out. Also, further insight into why I am the way I am.

Turns out that doctor knew a thing or two. Couple beers in, water breaks and back to the hospital they went.

My mom is a soldier. She opted for a natural child birth. It lasted seventy-two hours. I was just a cranium when I was born. Something it would take me eighteen years to grow into. My mother is a tiny lady. She s about average height but is small framed, much like myself. The fact that she gave birth to my 9 pound butterball looking ass without any painkillers is a medical miracle in and of itself. Sometimes I will see pictures of her from after my birth and be amazed that I didn t drag at least four feet of her intestines out with me or at least a spleen.

I had a perpetual double chin in all my baby pictures. Not that cute double chin that most babies have, mine was the result of 90% of my body weight being held in my head. My neck just was not strong enough to support the bowling ball that was perched on my spinal column.

I always see myself as a defective bobble head when I look at my baby pictures. You know when you play with a bobble head too much and the spring gets weak so the head just kind of flops around? Totally baby me.

For those of you who were not around in the early 80s, child safety was not exactly high on the priorities list for the world. Google Baby Jessica in the well and you ll see exactly what I mean. In those days most kids were lucky to be duct taped to the hood of the car let alone having to sit in a child safety seat until they hit puberty or whatever the law is now.

When I was a toddler, I spent most of my time in a blue bean bag chair or parked in front of the TV. We now know that you should never put an infant in a bean bag chair because they are notorious for bogarting the joint, drinking all your Steel Reserve, and bragging about their bitchin hacky sack skills. And, of course, there later was a study that too much television, too early in life would rot your brain. Do I begrudge my first time parents for doing either of those things? Fuck no, I love TV and bean bag chairs are comfortable as shit. Besides, if it wasn t for the homoeroticism of He-Man I would never have become the person I am today!

It was also a trend in those pre-child-safety-days for all playground equipment to be made as steel death traps placed on the hardest ground you could possibly find. This could either be concrete, popular in school yards and juvenile detention centers, or just good old Mother Earth, popular in most neighborhoods.

One particularly sunny day, one of the seventy-five you got in the Arctic Circle, my mother decided to take me to the playground that was near where we lived. Like most of the playgrounds of the era it was metal as fuck. I mean that literally, it was all metal, not in the way that one might say Jane Fonda is metal as fuck. I was walking at this point, I think, or I had bionic legs that propelled me around without the need for being carried.

How fucked would you be if your toddler had bionic legs? Like they re doing superhero shit like kicking doors in or dancing on the ceiling ala Lionel Richie?

Anyway, back on topic.

I saw other kids on the slide and decided that shit was for me. I had to go down that slide, see what the fuss was about. I have very little memory of the exactly what went down, but I do have flashes of details. I remember that the kid who went down on the slide ahead of me had on a green jacket. I remember that the playground was at the bottom of a small hill, kind of surrounded by houses. The rest I only know from secondhand accounts from my mom.

I climbed the ladder to the top of the slide with all the ease of a toddler without bionic legs. I m stood on the final rung just before you get to the flat part you sit on before you slide down, and I put my hands down to push myself up and then it all goes white. From what I understand, I let out a blood curdling scream. Turns out, metal playground equipment, a sunny day, and three-year-old hands are not a match made in heaven.

I had gotten third-degree burns on both hands from a playground slide. Some kids just touch hot stove tops; I had to one up all the other little bastards my age and become a statistic. It s not a particularly exciting statistic, 200,000 children a year are burned by hot playground equipment. So I ve got that in common with 199,999 other people, which is a pretty fun group to be in. You wouldn t know us outside of one defining characteristic. We re the assholes at coffee shops who insist on those stupid cardboard things they put around the cups to absorb some of the heat. We re the reason those stupid things exist. YOU RE WELCOME!

I don t think I can get away from the subject of dangerous playground equipment without mentioning the kid from Texas who, in 2017, was injured when a playground slide got so hot that it exploded. That s right, a playground slide exploded. Your kids aren t safe anywhere.

Because of this I ve always had kind of an odd relationship with my hands. My palms are constantly sweaty and my fingertips peel when the seasons change. There s no rhyme or reason for it, it just happens. On the plus side, I don t have fingerprints. Ok, I have fingerprints, but there aren t any ridges or anything in them. They just come off as smudges. You win some, you lose some.

When I was around 4 we moved out of the Snow Miser s asshole and down to my father s hometown in Alabama. My dad was stationed at a military town, which is technically in Tennessee, but considered Kentucky. I think? I m not 100% sure how that works, but it does.

About this same time, my mother was diagnosed with my little brother. They were better prepared this time. They had read all the books and made all the mistakes with me so there would be no bean bag chair or metal playground equipment for the new baby boy. They were seasoned pros at this shit.

My little brother and I were complete opposites. I with my red hair and blue eyes, definitely our mother s child and he, with his blonde curls and dark eyes, he looked more like our dad s side of the family. I used to think he was the WOOOOOOORST. Now that we re both adults that is actually so far from the truth, he s one of the coolest people I know.

This Easter Bunny is baked as fuck.

My brother is what most people would call the life of the party. And it s true, he makes friends wherever he goes, has a great roar of a laugh, and is really all light.

At some point after the birth of my brother, it was decided that we would move closer to where my dad was stationed. I assume a decision was made, I don t know. I was four; I don t really think my parents were consulting me on major life decisions at this point. Or at any point in my life really. Shit just kind of happens and I go along with it. I am a team player.

This is where the story takes a sharp turn into white trash town. We moved up to Tennessee and right into a double wide trailer that sat in an all gravel and red dirt trailer park. Now there s no shame in living in a trailer. You do you; live your life by any means necessary. Find what s comfortable to you. I don t judge. However, joining my family in our Natty Light dreams and KFC wishes was also my dad s sister, her husband, and their three kids. Including one who was just two and a half months older than my brother. We did not come to play with the other tenants of this trailer park. In case you were keeping count that s nine people in, if I remember correctly, a two bedroom trailer.

I remember only a couple things from my time in trailer town.

The first is getting in trouble for playing with one of my He-Man toys in the mud. I think I may have been getting in trouble more for playing in the mud than having the toy in the mud, but I distinctly remember the toy playing a major role in the scolding I received. I don t even remember which authority figure was mad at me, I just remember someone bigger than me was pissed. Looking back, I feel like given our current living situation they should ve been happy I was playing in the mud and not eating it. Maybe I was eating it. Shit, now I m going to have to reexamine my entire life and stop telling people I never ate mud because I was raised right.

I also remember once that I burnt my finger eating barbecue chicken. This only sticks out to me because somebody had made these cold compress things out of wash cloths; they were in the shape of a rabbit and held a single ice cube. It was pink and adorable. This was in the time before Pinterest was a major thing for white ladies, so I m sure it was something someone saw in Better Homes and Gardens or Southern Living or some shit like that.

The last thing I remember was I suppose the only Halloween we spent there. I was Big Bird that year. The costume was a plastic mask with eye holes and nose holes at the far end of the beak so the condensation from my breath ran down and dripped out so I looked like Big Bird with a coke problem. The rest of the costume was a shirt that was made from the same material as plastic grocery bags. The more I think on this costume the more I m almost positive that it was made out of asbestos and lead paint. It was the 80s, carcinogens were chic. Joe Camel was still a viable spokesperson. It s a wonder any of us made it through that decade without an extra toe.

Sometime shortly thereafter, we moved again to Virginia where bouncing baby boy number three was born.

My youngest brother is more like me, perpetually pissed off look on his face, a little standoffish, metal as fuck. I kid, the last thing you would describe me or any member of my family as is metal as fuck. But you get where I m going with this. My youngest brother is the smartest person I know. He s a savant at all things video games, he can sit down and beat a game in the same amount of time to decide what shape I want my pubes waxed. I can t even get through a section of this book without taking four coffee breaks and meandering around my apartment for two hours.

My Mom was a Pinterest lady before Pinterest existed.

By the time my youngest brother was born I was 5 and too fucking cool for school. It was almost the 90s; I would be starting kindergarten soon and had no time for an infant little brother. I was every book about siblings at every Scholastic Book Fair ever.

I was a brat. I can own that now that I m grown   And writing this on a computer that my mom bought for me. I was the oldest so there was no frame of reference for me to go off of. I only had the older brother tropes that 80s television had to offer. Michael P. Keaton didn t have time for Jennifer and I certainly didn t have time for my younger siblings.

Jesus, now that I think about it, somebody should have punched me in the mouth. By the time you re done with this book you may still feel compelled to do so. If you see me on the street and this part of the book makes you want to hit me, do it. I probably deserve it.

I was never outwardly mean to them, I just felt like I had better things to do.   Big boy books to read, worry about if I was going to get to hang out with the cool kids at school, act flippantly towards authority figures in the same way Zach Morris did because Mark Paul Gosselar was dreamy as hell and AC Slater could go fuck himself with that jheri curl mullet. He was rocking those crop tops though. Maybe I need to rethink my childhood crushes.

My brothers and I circa 1990-something

I d like to tell you a story about a time that I fell asleep on the bus and caused a near statewide manhunt when my mother called the state troopers.

I m almost positive that we were living in Virginia at the time and our house was literally across the street from the school I went to. No joke, our street and the school property were separated by a line of large hedges   They were possibly trees.

Look, I m going to be real with you guys for a second. My memory is shit and I drank a lot in the early 90s. I was really affected by the cancelling of *Blossom* and Kurt Cobain s suicide so I turned to the bottle.

None of that is true, except for the part about my memory.

Anyway.

For whatever, reason I had to ride the bus to school. Not my parents decision. There were these two brothers, actual siblings, not a gross way some white people would refer to two African American men, that also lived on my street and rode the bus with me to school. As is bound to happen sooner or later, one day they did not go to school and I was alone. I got to school fine. End game was the school so I didn t have to worry about not reaching my destination.

That afternoon, I got on the bus and one of the other kids tripped me, resulting in roaring laughter from all the other passengers. I was humiliated. As humiliated as a five-year-old could be I suppose. I booked it to my seat, curled up in a tiny ball, and willed myself not to cry. Who the fuck knows why, but mine was not the first stop on the bus route. So sometime between leaving the school grounds and getting to my stop, I had fallen asleep.

I woke up about the time the last person got off the bus, realizing that I had missed my stop, panicking because I had no clue where I was and I was alone on the bus with the driver. I emerged from my seat and nearly gave the driver a heart attack.

The reason I m telling you that story, is because that day I had decided that I was never going to be someone who was so unpopular that they got picked on. That never happened to the characters on TV, so I wasn t going to be the secondary nerd character. I was *not* going to be Screech Powers.

Except, I totally was Screech Powers.

As it turns out, I am not cool. Like not even in the slightest despite my best efforts. I was a terribly awkward child and an awkward adult too.

I always did my best to kind of ingratiate myself into the cool kids circle, but fly under the radar so that I didn t get kicked out or get my ass kicked. It basically worked for the better part of my life. Cuckoo in the nest mentality was my sword and shield all through school. That and a biting wit.

I was always of the mindset that you had to have a devil may care attitude like the super vanilla bad boys of TV. You would think I had absentee parents the way I make it sound like I was raised by Must See TV, but I can promise you that is so far from true. Being the first born, I was the tester kid. I was the one that they tried everything out on to see if it would work on the other two.

I was never incredibly rebellious; I didn t skip school until I was in high school for Christ s sake. Hell, I didn t start smoking until I was of age to legally buy cigarettes.

"He doesn't apply himself."

"He's not fulfilling the potential that we know he has."

That s teacher code for: Your son is lazy.

I was tested to be in the gifted program at like three different schools. Never made into any of them. I hate tests. I get bored and try to make designs on the Scantron answer sheets.

Was it laziness? Yeah, totally was. I enjoyed school more for the social interaction of it all. You know that scene in Mean Girls where

Lindsay Lohan is in the mall and all the teens turn into jungle animals? That s how I saw school. I watched the cool kids, emulated what they did, how they talked, how they dressed, thinking that maybe it would make me cool too.

Still to this day, I feel like most people tolerate me more than anything. I get it, though. I m annoying. I m with me 24/7/365 BELIEVE ME, I know what a pain in the ass I am.

When I was 12 or 13, I thought getting my ear pierced would put me on the cool kids radar. One of my mom s friends took me Claire s and we did it. I had a gold stud in my ear and was on my way to drinking virgin white Russians with the local biker gang or at least that s how it was going to go down in my head.

I have been told that line about white Russians and the local biker gang isn t all that funny. A virgin white Russian is a glass of milk. Don t think too hard on it.

Just like most of the things in my life, I didn t take care of it and had to take it out. I would try again years later to pierce my ears, but I looked like a giant douche canoe and took them out immediately.

When I was in Junior High, we were living in North Carolina. AOL was number one in the game for at home internet and anyone who was anyone was on it. You would instant message your BFF about the homework assignment you had that night or who was taking who to the only school dance of the year.

We had Prodigy.

Prodigy was AOL s bastard cousin. Super low-tech, none of the fun bells and whistles. No charming male voice announcing that you had mail. Just a screaming modem sound and a black and white background. It was yet another blow to my social standing or at least that s how I saw it. In reality, nobody gave a shit.

Junior High was also the time, like most pre-teen/teen boys, I went through my dirty phase. I didn t shower regularly, brushed my teeth only part of the week, only wore deodorant because my mother was surrounded by men and she would be damned if they smelled.

The worst part of the whole thing was that I got dandruff and by the time people started to notice it, I was too far gone to do anything about it. I was teased mercilessly for it and since then I swore that I would not be the dirty kid anymore.

Oddly enough, while I was the dirty kid I got my first real girlfriend. I forget her name, but she was this rail thin girl who went to my school. We went on a couple dates, movies, the mall, typical kid stuff. I don t even remember exactly how it ended, it had something to do with someone saying I was dating another girl behind her back and everything kind of went to shit after that.

Let me tell you, that there is no drama like middle school breakup drama. Battle lines get drawn, sides are chosen, and names are called, it gets fucking intense. That s exactly how it went down with this girl and me. Our classes lunch tables were right next to each other in the cafeteria so the tension was thick. Nasty looks were thrown over shoulders; people would bump chairs with Oh, I m sorry I didn t see you there! and then mutter an insult as they passed. It got so ridiculous at one point that neither of us were even involved in the sniping anymore, it was all coming from our classmates.

One night I decided that enough was enough; I would give her a ring on the phone and call a truce. This shit was getting ridiculous and even then I was tired.

I m going to mention being tired a lot. For reference, I ve been tired since 1984.

I called her house at a respectable time because I was raised right. If you re in the minority of people who don t remember actually having to call someone instead of texting allow me to enlighten you. A respectable time to call someone was after dinner but before nine o clock.

Moving on, I made the call and her mother picked up.

I should tell you that her mother was never my biggest fan. This stems from one night we were going to see the latest Michael Myers flick and when I walked into their house there was a Peter Gabriel music video playing on the television. In one shot of the video it shows a microscopic view of sperm. Oh look, sperm! I said with a laugh. I was obviously trying hard to impress this girl with my knowledge of all things reproductive. Tadpoles! her mother countered. I m sorry; ma am, but those are clearly sperm. We were all quickly ushered out the door and to the movie theater.

Back to the phone call.

Her mom picks up and I ask to speak to my ex. May I ask who is calling? Caller ID was a luxury item at this time. I told her who it was and her mother proceeds to tell me that I shouldn t be calling their house after I called her daughter a bitch and that her daughter didn t want to speak to me and then she hung up the phone. I was shocked that an adult had just told me off for something I did not do. I never once called her daughter a bitch. In my head, I had just called her mother one, but never her.

I recounted the story to my mom who was sitting nearby and she said that if that s how it was going to be then I didn t need to talk to that little tramp either. Cool. Mom s with me on this one.

A few minutes later, the phone rang. My mom picked it up, it was my ex. I took the phone, said hello, and she said You called? sounding completely exhausted with the idea of me. Your mother made it quite clear that you didn t want to talk to me, so I have nothing to say to you, I replied and promptly hung up the phone. Nothing in your life will ever feel as good as hanging up on somebody. Especially on a landline. Nothing.

The next day, I was called to the principal s office. Apparently old girl s parents had called the school and said that I had been harassing their daughter and calling her a bitch every time I saw her. The principal wanted to hear my side of the story. I was ready for this shit. My mom had coached me on exactly what to do if this situation arose. I looked the principal in the eye and said: I am not to answer any questions or say anything further until you call and speak with my mother.

So she called and explained the situation to my mother. I m not entirely sure what was said on my mom s end, but at one point in the brief exchange the color drained from the principal s face. The principal passed me the phone at which point my mom told me it was ok to talk and that she loved me.

I explained to the principal that I never once called her a bitch and that I had only called their house to put an end to the nastiness that was going on between our two classes and try to be friends with her, but her mother hung up on me so I retaliated when she called back minutes later.

The principal s advice was to just avoid each other in the future and not to speak to each other unless absolutely necessary. I was dismissed from the office with a pass to return to class.

Outside the office I saw my ex sitting in a chair waiting to go in. There were a million thoughts racing through my mind. Should I apologize for my classmates? Do I take the principal s advice and ignore her existence? My brain could hardly keep up with each new scenario I was running through.

In the end, when the office door clicked shut behind me, I looked her over one time and took a deep breath.

Bitch.

And ran off down the hallway back to class.

I remember when a kid in my neighborhood s dad came back from being stationed in Korea for a year; his parent s marriage fell to pieces. It was messy and within a week of his mom moving out, a new woman and her son had moved in.

Man that fucking sucks, I would think. Thank god that didn t happen when my dad came back from Korea.

Maybe a year, could be less, later my parents stopped sleeping in the same room. They claimed it was because my dad snored. It wasn t a lie, but it wasn t the whole truth either. I wasn t a stupid kid; I should have seen the signs.

Should I have seen it coming? Yes. Did I want to believe it was happening? No.

My mom started working again. She took a job at Bath & Body Works at the mall. My mom working wasn t a big deal. She had worked while I was younger up until, I think, right after my youngest brother was born. This didn t bother me; my brothers weren t sure how to function.

Next, my dad decided to take early retirement from the military and we were going to move back to his hometown in Alabama.

Again, this didn t faze me. Most of my life had been spent hopping from military installation to military installation. My youngest brother, however, had spent the majority of his life in North Carolina. He had started school in the same place and got to keep the same friends year after year. It was a luxury I was never afforded and the only time I ve ever been jealous of one of my siblings.

The final nail in the coffin came when it was announced that our mother would not be coming to Alabama with us. That she would be staying in North Carolina.

My brothers were devastated. I don t remember crying. I don t think I did. I shut down and I m pretty sure I just said Ok like I was being told that we were having chicken for dinner.

My parents divorce is one of the many things that I ve never truly and properly dealt with. I don t think I ll ever truly deal with it. It s so far gone in years that I don t really think about it. Maybe one day all the emotions I should have gone through that day will bubble up to the surface, but at that point it will probably kill me, so it s best not to think about that.

I don t blame either of my parents for ending their marriage because it was exactly that: THEIR marriage. My parents loved me and my younger brothers and that was really all that mattered. Whether they were together or not was just an extra plus, an add-on. Like guac at Chipotle.

Do I carry some resentment towards them for divorcing? I d be a liar if I said no. From time to time this resentment rears its ugly head at the most inopportune time. There s a bit of drama, an apology, and then it goes back to being buried in the deepest recesses of my chest. It s like in the X-Men comics when they explain that times of great stress cause the x gene to kick in causing a mutant s powers to expose themselves. That s kind of what my parent s divorce was for me. It was a moment that fractured my mental wellbeing. I was born mentally ill, I know that now, but that s when it first appeared, I think.

My dad and I didn t really know how to talk to each other outside of small talk which we both hate, so the fact that I wouldn t have my mom in my corner made me uneasy. Eventually my dad rekindled a relationship with a former flame from high school. There was a part of me that believed, and kind of still do, that this woman s soul goal in life was to cause a deeper rift in our relationship. Outside of the odd holiday, my dad and I wouldn t really speak. This went on for a period of several years. Things got better eventually. I think as we both got older we learned to appreciate each other for what and who we were rather than what we expected the other to be.

I have a better understanding of my dad now than I ever thought I would. I used to be bitter that he stayed in the Army and that we moved around so much, but I know now that he did it to provide for his family. I don t think he wanted to stay in the Army as long as he did which is why when he got the opportunity to retire early, he took it and never looked back.

I am very much my mother s child. In many more ways than that I look a great deal like her. In the process of writing this book, in looking back at my childhood with new eyes I can recognize my mother s struggle with mental illness and how much it mirrors to mine. My mother has the patience of a saint and I know that dealing with me as a child was no picnic and I have so much respect for her for that.

My mom s decision to stay in North Carolina was to give us the opportunity to get to know our dad better as he was away a lot while he was in the army. I admire anyone who is strong enough and brave enough to make a decision like that.

All grown up.

I Was Never on the Mickey Mouse Club
(Or: Don't Google Your Childhood Crushes)

The internet is a dangerous place for someone whose mind works like mine. It goes a million miles an hour and in fifteen different directions at once. So when I stumbled upon a *Buzzfeed* list of the hottest heartthrobs of the 80s and 90s, I fell into a rabbit hole of googling what all my childhood crushes were up to now.

It wasn t pretty.

What I got from the list is that if you were gonna be a Hottie McHotterson in the 80s and 90s you had to have blonde hair cut into an unfortunate bowl cut, blue eyes, and be named Joshua, Jackson, Jonathan, Jeremy or some combination of all four. Now I m thinking of using Jackson Joshua Jeremyson as my pen name. Really appeal to the people my age. I probably shouldn t do that though, they ll be really disappointed when they find out that I never dated Jennifer Love Hewitt or did heroin with one the Phoenix brothers.

Of all the heartthrobs from this time, Joseph Gordon Levitt is the only one that I could find that is still reasonably relevant and still fine as fuck. That boy grew up *RIGHT*! He started out as the adorable kid on *Third Rock from the Sun,* was an awkward teen in *10 Things I Hate About You,* and now he s supremely fuck-able in Um   That one thing he s doing now.

Looking at that list it occurred to me that we had mediocre taste in celebrity men back then. There s whole corners of the internet these days devoted to the sexiness of Neil Degrasse Tyson. Blake Shelton was just named as *People* magazine s Sexiest Man of the Year Ok, that s a terrible example, but you get what I m saying. Times and tastes have changed.

It wasn t even about talent back then, it was all about that doe eyed, sort of innocent boy you could take home to your mom. Like has anybody ever watched Devon Sawa in a movie and thought: That was an Oscar worthy performance. I was moved. No. Devon Sawa was a shit actor who was in a thousand movies because he was precious looking.

These days he looks like the college-aged guy who sells dumb high schoolers bags of oregano outside of house parties.

Another big creator of heartthrobs in the late 80s/early 90s was the Disney Channel s reboot of the Mickey Mouse Club, aptly renamed MMC. Because it was the nineties and abbreviations were cool I guess.

All the biggest music stars of the 2000s were cast members. You had Britney, Justin, and Christina. Hell, even Ryan Gosling was on that show.

I wanted to be on that show so bad, but I suppose everybody with extended basic cable did too. Only a couple of problems, I was too young and had no discernable talent. Not much has changed Except for being too young.

I wanted to be famous so bad when I was kid, didn t matter for what. I even went as far as to join the drama club at my elementary school because I thought that I would get discovered. That s actually not a joke, I legitimately thought that some big shot Hollywood producer was going to come to my elementary school, pluck me off the stage, and put me in movies.

Look, I m not saying that my portrayal of Santa Clause in the third grade class production of *This is Your Life Santa Clause* moved people to tears, but there were some people who were definitely misty eyed Or they could have just been bored to tears, whatever.

Just as another reminder of how desperately I wanted to be cool, once before school let out, I told everyone that I was travelling to Orlando to audition for the next season of MMC. Obviously that wasn t true, we were going to Alabama to visit my dad s family, but the people I went to school with didn t know that. Upon my return the following fall, clearly having not made the show, I told everyone that the show was being cancelled and they weren t accepting new cast members.

The year was 1993. MMC was cancelled in 1994. Maybe I should ve jumped on the Miss Cleo bandwagon while the getting was good.

Embracing My Crazy

I'm not usually this put together before 9 in the morning.

Buckle up kids, shit s about to get real.

I ve always been the type that when times get tough, I turn to stone. Being the oldest it was always kind of expected that I was the rock. I was the one who had to have his shit together at all times. So I did.

I would compartmentalize whatever emotion would show cracks in the façade and stay strong for the rest of my family. I ve done it in most situations.

I would later in life come to learn that this wasn t normal behavior and more along the lines of mental illness.

I had a pretty happy childhood. Aside from a few skinned knees there were no major speed bumps. We weren t lavishly wealthy, but we weren t dirt damn poor either. Clothes on my back, roof over my head, food in my belly; all that good shit that people take for granted.

It took me almost thirty plus years to accept that I am mentally ill. For the longest time it was chalked up to me being a moody teenager and then it was just that I was sensitive. These were the pre-Google days where we had to go to an actual doctor instead of just looking up symptoms on WebMD to find out that we were dying of First Corinthians whooping cough or something to that effect.

I feel like we should retire the whole BC/AD system and start using BG/AG (Before Google/After Google). Look at me! Just another millennial killing something that Baby Boomers love. Not that I m implying that I killed Christ   Or did I?

This was also a time before you could have an open dialog about your mental health without being told to suck it up or that you were just imagining things.   There is still a lot of stigma about mental health out there and quite a few people who refuse to believe it s real. But there is a dialog and there are people who are listening.

There are parts of my brain that don t fire the way other people s do. I m emotionally stunted. I have a tendency to self-destruct when things are finally going right for me. I m the proverbial bull in the china shop that is my life. I ve built a fortress of wit and sarcasm around myself not only to keep from getting hurt, but to prevent myself from letting everyone else down. If I keep everyone at arms length nobody gets hurt, nobody gets disappointed in me; it s a win/win for everybody involved.

I have days where all I want to do is clean and organize everything. There are days when it s a struggle for me to get out of bed. There are other days when I m in between those days where I think it would be easier to end it. Those days happen more frequently than I think anyone realizes or that I let on.

I m not constantly suicidal, but it is something that always sits in my periphery.

I carry all the emotions that I refuse to deal with in the center of my chest right behind my sternum. When I m really upset I get heart burn and that s where it hurts the worst. That s where my demons live. That s where my crippling self-doubt lives. That s the first place my brain goes when my self-esteem takes a nose dive. That s where my deepest fears become realized when a situation I can t control ultimately blows up in my face.

I imagine this place in my chest is a cupboard and the darkness that lives there is my boggart. Yes, just like in *Harry Potter*. I ve found that it s easier to cope with the worst parts of yourself if you compare them to something you enjoy thoroughly.

There s also the latent abandonment complex that causes me to cling to relationships. Be it friendships, intimate relationships, or working relationships I do everything I can do hold on to them. I can t shake that. It s weird because I was never abandoned by either of my parents. My parents were and are always there if I need them.

It stems from the fact that my mom stayed in North Carolina and that I m a momma s boy to the core. Do I tell my mother everything? No, but I tell her most things. A lot of things I never told her will end up in the pages of this book.

I live in this constant state of fear that the people I love the most will leave and I ll be well and truly alone. On the flipside of this, if someone gets too close I push them away and continue to push until they leave. Again, there are parts of my brain that don t fire the way others do.

I ve also learned that while struggling with mental illness you will seek other outlets to even out your brain s wonky chemistry. Some people gamble, some shop, and some paint. I turned to alcohol. I don t drink every day, but when I start drinking I have a hard time stopping. Chronic Binge Drinking is the proper term for it. It is usually at its worse when I would perform or in a social situation where alcohol was readily available.

Not understanding that I am mentally ill and then putting myself in a high stress situation such as performing or even hanging out at a bar with friends with the ever constant feeling that I didn t deserve these friends or that they d be better off without out me are the main factors that led to years of chronic binge drinking. I had to be the life of the party in order to keep people from realizing that I m less than I am and leaving.

This all came to a head in 2016 when I left the bar I was working at one night and got a DUI. It was a huge wakeup call that I had a problem. One that has now cost me a great deal of time, money, and the ability to drive legally. I m ashamed of myself because I knew better, but did it anyway.

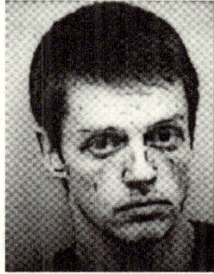

My actual mugshot.

That shame opened up new doors of feeling that I m a disappointment to everyone around me. For a while after it happened I contemplated suicide. I was so sure that everyone would be better off without my disappointing them at every turn. It took my friend, Scott, telling me to Buck up, we ll get you through this, to realize that I could climb this hurdle just as I had many others in the past.

You might be reading this and think: Hey that sounds like what I do! Or you might be saying: You are a crazy person! Either is fine. It s good to be able to relate to someone else s mental health struggles and I am, in fact, a crazy person so high five! An important thing to remember is that no one s mental illness is exactly the same. It manifests different in different people. The same can be said for self-care when you re having a bad mental health day. What works for me, might not work for you.

Little Things that Help Me through Bad Days:

1. Watch a movie. *Waiting to Exhale* is my go to when I just need to be in my feelings for a while. *Batman Returns* for when I need an

escape. *Love Actually* for anything else because it is a fantastic film.

2. Take super-hot or super cold showers. This helps me come back to my body when I start to dissociate. It reminds me that I am alive and start feeling again.

3. Just let it out. Scream, hit your pillow, cry, sing, dance, have sex, write, draw, sleep, create. Find an outlet and release everything you are feeling into it.

Self-care is important and it looks different for different people. Try lots of things until you find what works for you. Eventually you will be able to recognize when your mental health is taking a turn for this worst and start your self-care routine to soften the blow of the fall into the abyss. When you are eventually able to recognize when these dips into the black are coming, do your best to avoid being around those you care about. I say this because mental illness is not an excuse for being a shitty person and certainly does not give you a free pass. Be good to those around you because when things get bad, and they will, you will need a safety net.

For those that are reading this and are not affected by mental illness chances are someone close to you *is* and you may not know it. Ask how your friends and family are doing. Research signs of mental illness and watch out for them. The saddest thing is to hear relatives and friends of someone who has lost their battle with mental illness say: We had no idea. You won t have any idea if you don t ask. Don t press the issue, but be available and nonjudgmental.

Mental illness is scary because there is no cure and the thing that could kill you is yourself. That s why talking about it so important. So talk! Own your illness.

My mental illness is part of me, but it is not the only part of me. I embrace it fully, but I refuse to let that be the first thing you think when you see me.

I am first and foremost a world class asshole.

Church of the Red Yarn
(Or: How I'll Buy into Any Old Shit)

I ve always thought that organized religion was a joke. It just didn t make sense to me that some omnipotent being in the sky wanted you to act like a total fool to make it to some perfect kingdom in the clouds. That just sounds dumb And boring. If you have some sort of faith in your life I respect that, but I m not buying what you re selling, at least not where God and Jesus are concerned.

I kind of dig the pomp and circumstance of Catholicism. Only in the fact that it s high camp and so close to drag that it makes my gay heart swell. I don t support the Catholic doctrine or the fact that many of the men who wear their cloth are pedophiles; I just like the pageantry of it all.

The man who runs the Catholic Church wears special shoes and has enough jewelry to make any drag queen weep. I m really surprised that Catholicism isn t the official religion of homosexuals.

In the early 2000s every celebrity in the world started sporting these red yarn bracelets to go with their Von Dutch trucker hats and space-age metallic puffy jackets. Kabbalah was on the scene.

Kabbalah is an ancient form of Judaism that somehow mystically translates the bible. I think. I know there are ciphers and a tree of life; it s all very *Da Vinci Code*.

The minute that Britney Spears started rocking the red yarn, I was sold. This was my shit. I went out and bought all the books, even spent thirty dollars on a five inch piece of red string from the Kabbalah Center of Los Angeles. It was the dumbest shit ever, but I had found religion or at least a fad that made me seem cool in exactly nobody s eyes.

If somebody asked me about my red string, I went into this fifteen minute recitation of what was on the Kabbalah Center of Los Angeles website landing page. I was buying up Madonna s album

Music because she used some chants and I wanted to be right there with her, fake chanting and swaying my bony ass along to a catchy dance beat.

It last about six months. My commitment and the fad, that is. The minute I saw an interview where Britney started talking about her Southern Baptist faith, I was out. That thirty dollar piece of red string went straight into the garbage and who the hell knows where those books ended up. I ve probably still got them, books are expensive.

Like most white people at some point in their lives, I was also a Buddhist for about ten minutes. It lasted long enough for me to have to interact with an actual human being to realize that I was not cut out to turn the other cheek and meet opposition with love. I do not have the patience of a monk nor do I have the attention span to meditate. I m easily distracted so sitting and finding my inner peace for longer than thirty seconds is out.

For most white people, converting to Buddhism is more about colonization than it is finding inner peace. White folks *love* to try shit that s been around for thousands of years and then act like they discovered it. The term for it is Columbusing. I, however, only decided to give it a go after I watched *What's Love Got to Do with It*. When Tina shows up at Jackie s house and learns about Buddhist chanting, I was hooked. If Buddhism was good enough for Angela Bassett as Tina Turner then it was good enough for me.

While I still have your attention, does anyone else find the signs outside of churches incredibly irritating? Even the ones that turn into memes and end up on Facebook kind of grate my nerves. I have this dream of one day going around to various churches and swapping the G in God with a Z . If I get really lucky on that particular night I ll come across one that says Kneel before God which will then become Kneel before Zod.

Zod is a character from the Superman comics and films, for those who don t immediately get the reference. Hilarity will ensue, I m sure of it.

I read up on Scientology once, but turns out that is a fucking cult and some of the craziest shit in the world. Also, I m poor and couldn t afford the dues. I tell people I m a Scientologist as a joke, it s even on my Facebook as my preferred religion. It s not.

Tom Cruise has probably put a hit out on me for this chapter. It was nice knowing you all.

On That Gay Shit

The Gay Agenda starts off with a healthy breakfast.

I ve always known that there was something about me that was different. I was not like the other boys in my school or in my neighborhood. I had no interest in sports. After the age of seven I was shit at video games. I never paused a taped episode of Baywatch to try to get a glimpse of Pamela Anderson s nipple. Y all did that shit in the 90s; don t even try to deny it.

Those boy things never appealed to me in the way they did others.

I was probably thirteen when I first started to realize that I was attracted to other guys. It wasn t some great Oprah aha moment; it was just one of those things that was like: Shit he s fine.

I had a type back then. My crushes were always athletes and they always played basketball or soccer. That was it. If you were a boy that went to my junior high school and you played basketball or soccer you more than likely turned up in my early masturbatory fantasies.

My first ever hardcore crush was on a boy that lived across the cul de sac from us in North Carolina. His name was Calvin. Calvin was like a foot taller than me, played basketball and football, and played the trombone in our school s band. And the big winner for me was that he always smelled nice.

Somethings to note as we move forward with this story: First, we were living on a military base. Second, this is happening in the late 90s when I wasn t aware of any form of gay culture.

I didn t know how to approach my first same sex crush so it was business as usual as far as I was concerned. We were friends I guess. We walked to the bus stop every morning together. We went to the movies. I went to his football and basketball games. Christ, I was living a gay coming-of-age movie before I realized such a thing existed. I was basically living the plot of *Get Real* only without the reciprocation. If you haven t seen *Get Real,* I highly recommend it. I mean, like most gay films, it s terribly acted, but there s some heart there.

Anyway.

To avoid getting the ever loving shit beat out of me, I stayed friends with Calvin. Never made any mention of this blossoming imaginary romance I had plotted out in my head for us, where we would buy a luxurious cabin in the mountains of North Carolina and raise standard poodles. I kept that shit to myself. Like I said earlier, I wasn t a stupid kid.

Sometimes my mind drifts to Calvin. So I google him. Just to see how he is, what he s up to, if there are any standard poodles involved.

And then I google myself for a half hour afterwards because shit he s still fine.

Fast forward to high school. I am owning this gay thing. Ok, not really owning, but I knew enough to get from point A to point Butthole, if you know what I mean. I was still academically lazy and kind of a loner. Oh, and I wasn t just gay in high school; I was a *theater gay*. Yeah, I know theater gays are the worst; you don t have to tell me.

Given that my life is a poorly written gay teen comedy, I also had a secret boyfriend. He played soccer and baseball (Still had that type, only this time I lowered my standards to include baseball players). I say he was a secret because nobody at school knew we were together and by together I mean giving each other fumbling hand jobs anytime the opportunity presented itself. It was my freshman year, Queer as Folk hadn t premiered yet, so I had no idea what I was doing. Come to think of it *Queer as Folk* wasn t really a great guide book to gay sex either.

Looking back on my early days of sex, I am mortified. That couldn t have been pleasurable for anyone involved. I hadn t even discovered that wonder that is coconut oil yet, so I know my hands were rough as fuck. Oh well, closet case first boyfriend sandpaper hands were probably his thing. Probably still is. I don t know his life or his wife. I don t Google this one.

Remember that story I tell people about my conception? This is where it comes back into play.

I lost my virginity in the back of a pickup truck. Not extended cab pickup truck backseat. In the bed of a navy blue, Chevy pickup truck. It had a lift kit, those naked lady mud flaps, and a bumper sticker that read: My other ride is your mom.

If you ve ever had anal sex, you know that there is *a lot* of prep work that goes into it. I didn t do any prep work. Hell, at the time, I didn t know that you were supposed to do any preparation. I m better versed in the ways of gay sex now, but then Not so much.

There s a supposedly haunted playground in the town I went to high school in. That s where we decided it would go down. Apparently I was tired of my life being a gay teen comedy and went straight to wanting it to be a horror movie.

My first time was all the things that first times are supposed to be. It was painful, it was awkward, embarrassing. It lasted exactly twelve and a half minutes.

I can hear the wheels in your brains turning. You re asking questions about the lack of preparation. Let me put your thoughts at ease; I did not shit on his dick. I have never shat on anyone s dick. I have learned that nobody likes a dirty bottom and so if I m gonna bottom my ass will be clean enough to eat   And I hope you do!

We didn t last much longer. When you re an athlete in a small-ish Alabama town, once you put your penis into another man I guess it s a little hard to make eye contact on a regular basis.

Also, fuck you Daniel, I m a great lay!

I wouldn t come out until a year or so later. To my mom. Outside of a Pizza Hut. I am nothing if not classy.

I m trying my best not to describe myself as not like other gays, but it just sounds like I m saying I m not like other Moms, I m a cool Mom.   Which I guess is almost exactly the same sentence.

Ways I Am Not Like Other Gay Men:
1. I do not like Lady Gaga or Taylor Swift. (Lady Gaga is problematic as fuck. She hung around people in black face in Germany and has yet to apologize. Taylor Swift is the epitome of a white feminist and her music is garbage.)

2.

Shit, I thought there would be more to that list. So maybe I m just like other gays? I probably need to market myself differently.

"I'm just like other gays only cool." No, that won t work either; I am the most uncool person you ll ever meet.

"Diet gay! Now with less stereotype!" Nobody will buy that, I did drag.

"I'm here! I'm queer! I'd really like a nap!" That sounds like everyone I know.

"I'm gay. Yes, really. Oh, you were being sarcastic." THERE IT
IS!

You know what I really love? Pride celebrations! A weekend long
party that s all about being an LGBTQIA+ person? Fuck yeah, I m
there!

One of my favorite pride memories was walking around Piedmont
Park in Atlanta with a group of my closest friends, drinking
Everclear and lemonade out of a large Subway cup, then hiding in
plain sight behind a vendor tent and sniffing poppers. That sounds
trashy as fuck, but my god that was a good weekend.

That was also the weekend that I met Cazwell at Jungle. He smelled
so good, even after he had come off stage and was covered in sweat.
After I got a picture with him my hand was covered in his sweat and
I may or may not have licked it off my hand in the parking lot.

I didn't fuck him... But I thought about it!

I kind of look like Sigourney Weaver in *Alien: Resurrection* in that
picture. Y know the one where she s been cloned using the aliens
DNA and the whole movie is just terrible? No? Just google it and
then come back to this picture and you ll totally catch the reference.
If you did get that reference I hope you re laughing with me.

If you ever want to see a gay man freak the hell out and go through a

mid-life crisis right in front of your eyes, tell him that he s not a
 new school gay anymore. It happened to me not too long ago.

It s something that I ve kind of embraced. I m a thirty-something
gay man who knows the struggles of those who came before him. I
remember the times when Wilson Cruz was the only out gay
character on TV, when watching *Queer as Folk* was done in secret,
when Ryan White died. The baby gays of today have it easier than
we did, just as I had it easier than the gays that came before me.

I do have a few questions for the baby gays of the world. Why no
socks? What do we have against socks? On the flipside, why socks
with Birkenstock sandals? Also, what is so great about Lana Del
Rey? Why are we calling everybody Mom? Why don t you know
that there are fifty pennies in a roll? Does everyone need a YouTube
channel? Why don t you get my 2007 Britney references? *WHY
ARE YOU SO YOUNG AND PRETTY?!?!?!?*

Sorry for the yelling, I m an old gay. I think it s what we do. This is
new territory for me.

If you were hoping for some sort of profound It Gets Better
moment from this chapter you will, once again, be disappointed. I m
not saying that it doesn t get better, because it does   Eventually
At some point   I m still waiting.

Easy, Breezy, Beautiful… Barely Fooling Anyone
(Or: My Love Letter to Atlanta Drag)

All drag queens look mad all the time because we haven't peed for three hours.

I should preface this chapter by saying that I hardly consider myself a drag queen in the traditional sense. I m not glamorous, I m not really all that funny, and let s be real, I m not fooling anybody with my illusion. I d more consider myself a drag clearance section. My drag aesthetic now is somewhere between Jane Hathaway from *The Beverly Hillbillies* and Dead Sex Worker #4 on *Law & Order: SVU*. I hope that gives you a frame of reference before going into this chapter thinking you re about to be regaled with stories of a super glamorous eight foot tall drag queen. I m right under six feet tall in heels and I don t like to wear wigs because they re hot, give me headaches, and I usually look like a drowned rat.

To Wong Foo, Thanks for Everything, Julie Newmar was my first taste of drag culture. It was 1996 or 97 the first time I saw the movie. On VHS to be exact. Sign of the times and what not.

Before I go any further, can we talk about how inaccurate *To Wong Foo* is? Anyone who knows anything about drag (and that s a lot of people now. Thanks RuPaul!) knows that it is not comfortable. It s certainly not travel across the country in a convertible comfortable. There s body parts pushed into places they shouldn t be, things are synched, there s duct tape involved, it s hot, it s not something for extended wear. But here we have Patrick Swayze, Wesley Snipes, and John Leguizamo doing just that. I m not hating on the film, because it s one of my favorites and it was so important because at the time the only gay representation in media we had was Ellen and Ricki Vasquez on *My So Called Life*.

Also, can we talk about the lack of contour in that movie? No. Ok, I ll move on.

I was working at a restaurant attached to a gay bar in Nashville. I would go out with my coworkers after the restaurant closed and watch a drag show. This would be the first time I would look at a drag show and say to myself I could do that.

It wouldn t be until later, when I would say that out loud, that someone finally said Alright, nut up or shut up.

I was living in Atlanta at the time, working in this pseudo hippy pizza joint. *RuPaul's Drag Race* was in its third season. Every Wednesday we had charity drag queen bingo. The host of drag queen bingo was a foul mouthed, bearded monster by the name of Ruby Redd. Ruby is a no holds barred, drinks tequila like its water, cross between Joan Rivers and Paul Bunyan.

I was in love.

One night during bingo, I made some passing comment about maybe wanting to perform one Wednesday and one of the other servers dragged me over to Ruby and the rest, as they say, is history.

I started my drag career as a charity queen which basically means I wasn t getting paid. Any show that I did was for some organization that relied on donations to make things happen. I was basically paying out of pocket for drag at the time with no return on my investment. I was raking in the good karma so I was just adding bricks to my house in the great beyond.

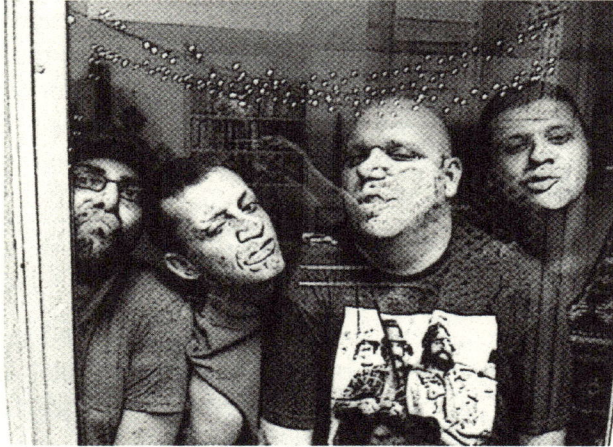
Redd Family Photo.

I was heavily influenced by Raja, the winner of season three of *Drag Race*. Later, I would be heavily influenced by Sharon Needles, but that would pass when I found out that she is a racist dumpster fire. Early in my career I was the queen who didn t wear pads or hair. You couldn t tell me SHIT! I thought I was the be all, end all, current reigning queen of Atlanta drag.

I started out performing twice a month doing songs that were off the beaten path for most queens at the time. I tried to stay away from anything that was Top 40 at the time; I was doing songs in other languages, and tried to peg myself as Atlanta s dark and broody queen.

It worked for a time. Slowly but sure I started to realize that in order to make money for these organizations, and later in my career myself, that I would have to bend a little on my rule about no Top 40 music.

With the addition of performances to Wednesday night bingo, the popularity began to grow so I started performing weekly.

Enter Marcella.

Marcella was one of my coworkers at the pizza place who soon began performing with me on Wednesdays. She adopted Ruby s signature bearded beauty look and was basically the antithesis of everything I was as a performer. Marcella and I would get spectacularly drunk, perform, and then go to one of the bars all the while acting like we ran that town. Again, you couldn t tell us SHIT!

Marcella and I in the early years.

Marcella is still the antithesis of everything I am except that she is a nine-foot-tall goddess and such a better drag queen than I am!

The hangovers from those early days are almost as good as the memories of two busted ass baby queens in high whore drag prancing around Midtown Atlanta like we had just come off winning *Drag Race.*

It wasn t long into our tenure as the featured, only, performers of *Birdcage Bingo with Ruby Redd.* That Ruby told us it was time we took her last name. We were Redds! We were a force of nature. Ruby was the mouth, Marcella was the talent, and I was the wild card. I finally felt like I was a part of something. I felt invincible.

Being Ruby s daughters afforded us opportunities most fledgling queens only dream of. Any time Ruby hosted an event, if there was room for performers, we were there. The exposure was fantastic.

I quickly became known in Atlanta for a few things.

1. My lip syncs were always pretty tight.
2. My Annie Lennox impersonation was/is pretty spot on. Except I play my Annie a little more manic than she actually is in real life.
3. Getting blackout drunk and walking off stage with two or three minutes left in the song.

There is an explanation for the last item on that list. I suffer from near debilitating stage fright. Before any show, I am a bundle of nerves and anxiety. Alcohol became a coping mechanism; one that I would not recognize as such for many years. It took the edge off and allowed me to do something I love. On the downside, alcohol gets you drunk and makes you do dumb shit   Who knew?

If you are thinking of becoming a drag performer, I highly suggest starting in Atlanta. There is a wealth of knowledge on the craft and an army of seasoned performers who are ready, willing, and able to help.

It s amazing to me, knowing what I do of the queens in Atlanta, that there are many who think that Atlanta queens are catty, mean, and self-serving. This is a lie and anyone who says so should be put in a time out. You know nothing, Jon Snow! In my entire time as a performer in Atlanta, I never once met a queen who didn t want to help or had a piece of advice to take you to the next level.

There are a few shady queens in Atlanta, if I m being honest. That s a given, but it s not as bad as some folks want to make it out to be.

Baby queens out there, my advice to you is this: *LISTEN!* Listen to the seasoned queens. Be a sponge for their knowledge. They ve been there and done that. You won t get anywhere if you don t listen. Trust me.

I was and still am a stubborn queen. I want to do everything my way, play by my rules, and do it all without any help.

Several years ago, I was doing a competition at a bar that I also had a weekly show (Thank you very much!). It was hosted by Phoenix, of *Drag Race* season three fame, and featured some of the most talented performers in the world as judges. I went into this competition thinking that I was going to win because I different from the other performers.

Marcella and I both decided to enter this competition. Other performers lost their minds. It will destroy your friendship, they said. I would never compete against my sister, they said. Anytime we went into something where there was a chance the other would not be selected there was never a competition aspect between us. If you ever see Marcella and I perform at the same show you ll see why. Needless to say none of their fears came to light. Just as we both knew they wouldn t.

I did not win.

I was voted off during the Las Vegas Showgirl themed week. Still to this day, I have no idea what kind of number I could have done to stay in the competition past that week. That theme throws me for a fucking curve ball. I am grateful to Phoenix and the judges because they did make me think outside of the box.

Coincidentally, the week I was voted out was the same week Marcella was brought back into the competition. She did extremely well. But she wanted it more than I did. Marcella has a hunger for drag that I just don t have.

After being voted out, I felt like I had cheated the other contestants who were not as fortunate as I was to have a weekly show and I was a little bitter because I had forced myself to jump through hoops for a panel of judges when I thought my art should speak for itself. I made a Facebook post that night I was voted off that said I was glad to be voted off because it was a weight lifted off my shoulders and I realize now how much of an asshole that made me sound because I auditioned to be a part of that show. I freely admit I am an asshole, but the wording of that post is terrible and I regret that. I doubt

Phoenix will ever read this, but if by chance she does, thank you for the opportunity!

It s almost every queen s dream to be cast on *RuPaul's Drag Race*. It s what most work towards. At one time, it was mine too. Five years into my time as a drag performer I can tell you that I am not built for drag competitions. I admire the queens who work and hone their craft to be able to do drag fulltime and travel the world, but once again I m a lazy queen.

There are a lot of expectations of people when they hear you were a drag queen in Atlanta, especially when you are trying to get bookings at other bars outside of Atlanta. I am the opposite of what Atlanta drag is touted to be. I usually go in for the hard sell which usually ends with I put out. I ve never actually had to sleep with anyone to get a booking, but I m certainly not above it. That ll probably be the opening quote for my E! True Hollywood Story should I ever get that famous. I won t.

If you are ever in Atlanta and want to check out some quality drag queens and shows. Here is a list of queens that you should track down and see:

1. Ruby Redd at *Birdcage Bingo with Ruby Redd.* Wednesday nights at The Hideaway
2. Marcella Grrleen Redd
3. Celeste Holmes
4. Dax!
5. Taylor Alxndr
6. Evah Destruction
7. Every drag queen in Atlanta   Except that one. You ll know her when you see her.

Really just go see any drag show in Atlanta. There are literally hundreds happening on any given night. Tell em River sent ya!

Actually, don t tell them I sent you, you ll probably get thrown out and stuck with a tab that I ve left open for five years.

We should probably talk about the elephant in the gay bar. The drunken, stumbling, grabby handed, screaming elephant in the gay bar. That s right; I m talking about straight women. Y all need to learn to act right in a gay bar and at a drag show.

I don t mind straight women at the bar or watching the show, but calm down. Don t touch the drag queens. Stop trying to dance with me, the smell of White Diamonds makes me gag. Nine times out of ten, we don t mind you being there. We want your money just as much as everybody else s, but when you start to make a spectacle of yourselves then we ll have to have you removed.

FAQs Drag Queens Are Tired of Hearing from Straight Women:

Q: Where is your penis?
A: The same place it always is, just tucked away until Christmas.

Q: Will you do my makeup?
A: If you pay a drag queen to do your makeup they absolutely will. Otherwise, watch YouTube makeup tutorials like we did.

Q: My significant other wants to have a threesome; will you come in drag and be our third? (Hand to God, this was actually asked of me!)
A: Maybe. What does your significant other look like?

There are probably thousands of other questions that have been posed to other drag queens, post your favorites in the comments below. Oh wait, this isn t a YouTube video. Disregard.

On the flipside of this, gay men please stop grabbing non-men s titties. Like really, stop! That s sexual assault even if you meant nothing malicious by it.

In every queen s career they want to earn a really cool tag line that is said before they re brought on stage. Things like: the body beautiful, or the large and in charge, or from RuPaul s Drag Race. I, too, wanted a cool tag line and eventually I got one.

Please welcome to the stage… Probably not sober… River Redd!

Somebody asked me recently what my least favorite memory of doing drag was and I probably said something stupid and noncommittal like I don t have one or that all my drag memories are great blah, blah, blah, I d like to thank the Academy. But the truth is there is one that stands out.

One of the gay magazines in Atlanta was holding a contest much like you see in most other larger cities where the readers voted on who their favorite drag queen is. It s common place in most metropolitan areas with a thriving gay community. The difference in this one was that once the top ten were voted on there would be a performance competition and the winner would receive the title Queen of Queens and some cool prizes or some bullshit like that. At the time I was a very busy queen. Marcella and I were doing like four shows a week, we were both working full time, and so I paid very little attention to it at the start.

We were both nominated.

Once the nominations were over, I was very vocal on social media that anyone and everyone should vote for anyone but me. I, honestly, wanted no part in it and I know that sounds ungrateful to whoever nominated me, but stuff like that has always felt a little gross to me. I m not unappreciative, but at the same time I d rather you didn t vote for me in an online poll. Plus, there were other queens in the city who were far *FAR* more deserving of this particular opportunity than I was.

For all my begging and pleading for people not to vote for me, I ended up in the top ten and was expected to show up to perform. Which I did. I m never one to turn down the opportunity to perform. But I made sure to pick a number that would ensure I wouldn t win. I picked the weirdest number I had in my stable and sure enough the winner was someone who is 1) a much better performer than I am and 2) deserved it.

Drag has allowed me to meet some really cool people and do some really cool things. Will everyone s experience mirror mine? Fuck no; I m a lucky bastard who just happened to be in the right place at the right time. But I think everyone should try drag. No matter your gender, do it! Even if it s just for Halloween or a friend s birthday party.

I m sort of retired now. I guess retired isn t really a good word for it. I don t actively seek out bookings like I used to. If I m asked to do a show, I totally will, but I don t go out of my way to try to be on cast anymore. I miss doing it all the time, but knees ain t what they used to be and walking in heels puts me out of commission for about forty-eight hours.

Go support your local drag performers; you ll be happy you did!

No Fats, Femmes, or Asians... Add Lettuce and Tomato

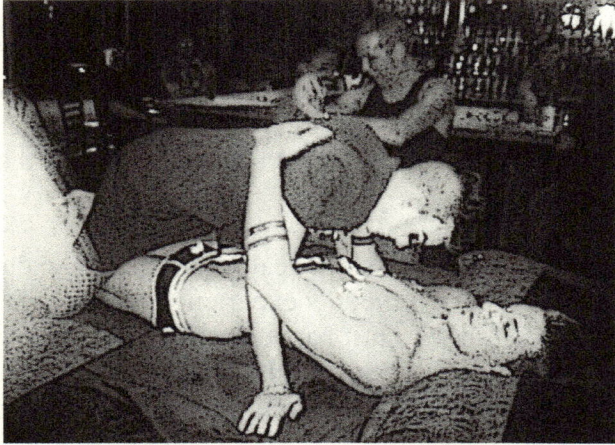

You ever drank Peach Schnapps out of an actual fuzzy navel? Because I have.

I love a good ho story. Doesn t matter who it s from or who it was with, if you got a ho story I ve two ears ready to listen.

You: Guess whose dick I just sucked?
Me: Bitch, who?

I will never turn down a good ho story.

As I sit here in front of my computer thinking about what to write in this chapter, it occurs to me that I don t know much about hookup culture before smart phones. I know Craigslist was (is?) pretty popular, but like what did our gay forefathers and mothers and gender nonbinary people do in the dark times before smart phones?

It occurs to me that they actually had to talk to each other. How difficult that must have been. Now all you gotta do is hit somebody with a Looking? and then a dick pic and Wham! Bam! You re getting laid. What a time to be alive!

I have a love/hate relationship with Grindr. I like the unsolicited dick pics. It makes me feel like Dian Fossey. Penises in the mist! I am an anthropologist of the cock. Trust me when I say I have seen some dicks y all. Not all of them are pretty, not all of them are big like porn would have you believe, but they are out there and they are hard and they deserve to be sucked just like any other penis!

As someone who is on Grindr, I never really understood the obsession with Masc4Masc or No fats, no femmes, and no Asians or even more prevalent and as equally disgusting: No rice, no spice, no chocolate. Why would you want to close yourself off from ALL our community has to offer?

First of all, I have never had a poor sexual experience with an Asian nor is it true that all Asian people have tiny dicks. I hooked up with an Asian guy who literally beat the breaks off of it when we were together. He was packing and knew exactly how to work it. Caused me to walk funny for days afterwards. Don t pass on some shit like that!

Fat people will fuck with you and then feed you! Everybody loves food, it s essential to life. Free food tastes better. So like why would you not want to fuck a fat person? Also, it s really gross to body shame somebody who doesn t have six pack abs or fall in the Fiona Apple weight class especially when you re both just trying to get your rocks off.

Gender nonconforming people are the unsung heroes of the LGBTQIA+ community. Anybody can walk around in a tank top and show off their killer triceps, but to fully live your truth like a gender nonconforming person does when it could literally get them killed? That s fucking bravery. I applaud them; y all are the true MVPs and fuck anybody who doesn t want to bask in your glory in an intimate setting.

If any part of your Grindr/Scruff/Growlr/Prowlr/Blendr etc., profile talks about how you have a preference for only white guys. You re a racist. No, no, this is not open for debate or argument, it s my book, and this is the truth. White people have put black people through so much and for you to cast them aside for not looking like you or to say I have black friends, I just wouldn t fuck a black person, is tokenism and it s gross. Do you know how much we owe to black people? If it weren t for black people we wouldn t know about bathing on the regular. If it weren t for black people I would never have learned about the magic that is coconut oil. I m not saying you have to go out and pity fuck a black person, but don t exclude a person because of the color of their skin. Address your racism, educate yourself, and do better.

I m one of those people on Grindr who is adamant about seeing a picture of you before we start talking. I just like to know who I m talking to. I don t regularly have conversations with sunset views of the ocean or the rims on a Maserati so I don t feel like it s asking too terribly much to ask to see your face. I get it if you re super private or you re not out at work, but I live in Alabama, I don t work for TMZ, I m not in the business of outing people. What you do in the privacy of your own home is none of my business. However, if you are a married dude cruising Grindr for some dick, I will ask you point blank if your significant other knows. I am not a homewrecker and I certainly do not think it is fair for you to put your spouse in a position to possibly contract an STI because you re out getting your dick sucked by Bobby with the cold sores.

For the love of all that good and right in this world, gays, I implore you to stop using clean when referring to HIV and STI status. There is nothing dirty about an HIV positive person. They have enough going on to have to deal with your closed minded ass. If a person is Positive Undetectable that means you cannot contract it from that person. There is enough division and segregation in our community without you creating more because you deem someone who is positive to be less than a person.

I have to take a minute to give props to the power bottoms out there. Y all are really out there doing the Lord s work. A few questions though. Do you douche every day? I know some power bottoms who take dicks at the drop of a hat. If I m gonna bottom, I gotta know like two or three days in advance so I can avoid eating at Moe s, douche like seventeen times, and start fasting. What do y all eat? Bottoming is tricky enough, but like are you on an all liquid diet, are there protein shakes specifically marketed to the power bottom set?

Some of y all take these hookup apps way too seriously. Sex should be a fun activity between two consenting adults. It s cool to have a type but if your type excludes a marginalized group, might be time to rethink your life choices. Am I saying that you should fuck anyone and everyone who hits you up? No, there isn t enough time in the day and you have laundry to do. Might even think about cleaning your selfie mirror.   What I am saying is broaden your horizons. Try new things. Be safe out there. Make smart choices.

Do no harm, but take no shit!

Author's Note: *If your name is Bobby and you sometimes get cold sores, I am so sorry. I promise this was not a personal attack on you; it was just the first name that popped into my head. You're beautiful and I love you.*

I've Got Beef with People Magazine

If you are of a certain age, you will remember a time when *People* magazine was a reputable source for celebrity information. It taught us such things as: George Clooney s waxing routine, who famous people go to for the best high colonics, or which baboons asses were sacrificed to make Julia Roberts lips. None of these were actual stories ran in People magazine   To my knowledge.

People used to be cover to cover of wholesome celebrity news, the occasional national headline, and a really easy crossword puzzle.

I m not really sure when it happened, but sometime in like the past five to ten years the back half of *People* magazine has been about regular people. Not even regular people who have had interesting run-ins with celebrities, just normal every day folks losing weight, teaching their pets sign language, lame shit like that.

I don t know how to break this to the fine editors at *People*, but NOBODY FUCKING CARES ABOUT NOT FAMOUS PEOPLE!!!! More importantly, I m not paying six dollars for thirty pages about celebrities, a crossword puzzle, and twenty pages about normal everyday folks.

Let me just cut to the quick, if something is titled Every Day Heroes I am immediately disinterested. I don t agree with rewarding someone with a photoshoot and four page spread in a nationally syndicated magazine just because they re a good fucking person. Oh you gave a homeless person a sandwich? Good fucking job on being a decent person, Karen. I m not going to applaud you for that shit and neither should *People* magazine.

I don t read that magazine anymore and neither should you   Unless I m featured in it one day at which point you should buy multiple copies.

That last statement isn t entirely true. I *should* say that I don t read it unless there is Royal wedding coverage.

Fear of the Uncircumcised Penis and Other Sexual Misadventures

Power
Bottom
Starter Kit

I love sex. I ve got a dick; sex is on my mind constantly. I m not ashamed of it. Have I had a lot of sex? Not a lot. Have I had more sex than say the average person? More than likely. Am I good at sex? Meh, I wouldn t say good. Sex with me is like a game of Jenga It s gonna fall apart quick.

I didn t see my first uncircumcised penis until I was 21 or 22. I was at a New Year s Eve party and this guy who was a friend of a friend of a friend had gotten ridiculously drunk and dragged me into an upstairs bathroom. There was some heavy making out against the bathroom door, some grinding, some pre-second base action happening.

You sure you want to do this?

I was already on my knees with his belt in my hand, what the hell kind of question was that?

I pulled his pants down in one swift motion because I do not fuck around and came face to face with his penis. I jerked back a bit. I had never seen one in a turtle neck before. Before I could explain my inexperience to him, he kind of twisted his body away from me and then twisted back really fast causing his dick to hit me in the eye.

 Yeah, you like that shit don t you?

I had just been assaulted by a penis in a Brooks Brothers sweater set, liking that was the furthest thing from my mind. Yeah, if we could not do that again, I d like that even more.

For the record, if you spend more than two minutes examining a dick, trying to figure out the logistics of what to do, it s going to kill the mood. Awkward, party of one, right here!

I pulled some bullshit lie out of my back pocket and told him that because I had been drinking I didn t think I could orally pleasure him the way I would like so maybe we should try something else.

Color me surprised when he bent over the sink and looked back over his shoulder and slurred Have at it!

We ended up breaking a soap dish that night. Being a good guest, I left a twenty dollar bill on top of the broken pieces along with a note that said I hoped that was enough to cover the damage and that I had a lovely time. Couldn t wait til next year!

I wouldn t say I m an expert now with uncut dick, but I do know my way around the foreskin.

I used to fuck around with this one dude that my friends and I nicknamed Squidward, yes like the *SpongeBob* character Actually, y know what? I m gonna save this story for another time. If I take the time to explain why we called him Squidward I ll look gross and it s better that I spare you.

Moving swiftly and professionally forward

There used to be a charity event in Atlanta called Big Gay

Gameshow. The way it would work is local gays of note, and sometimes bigger gay names, would compete in recreations of 70s style gameshows. They did Family Feud, Match Game, and a few others that I can t remember right now. It was loads of fun to watch and be a part of. They should bring that back.

Once they brought in someone who I wouldn t say was particularly a star, but people knew who he was. He was in that weird semi-celebrity area of almost fading from memory to almost making a comeback. If I said his name, you d know who I m talking about and that description would make complete sense.

After the Big Gay Game Show, he was being shown around town by a couple of drag queen friends of mine and a gaggle of hangers on. Marcella and I were hanging out at Burkhart s that night. I can t particularly remember what was happening that night, but I remember that there were a lot of people at the bar for it to be the middle of the week.

We ran into the pseudo-celebrity, our two friends, and their entourage and decided to tag along. The dude was buying drinks and wherever there was free alcohol I was gonna follow. Although I will admit now that I did have ulterior motives. I had the idea that this guy would be my in. For what? No clue, but I was gonna go for it and if I had to fuck my way to the top so be it.

The exact details of what happened before we got back to his hotel room are a bit fuzzy as he was feeding me Rumple Minze shots and that never ends well. At some point we lost Marcella, we ended up at a strip club, and then from there he pulled me into a cab and off into the night.

You don t know awkward until you are being held like a napping baby in the back of a yellow cab. Before going to the hotel, he had the driver stop at Waffle House. He ordered his food, I didn t order anything nor did he offer. Top notch gentleman this one. On the plus side, he blew me in the Waffle House bathroom so I guess the night had that going for it.

Back at his hotel, he inhaled his Waffle House order and started force-feeding me his tongue. He had syrup in his beard and now whenever I smell maple syrup and tea tree oil I cringe.

The sex was as good as you can probably expect from someone who I would later find out was coked out of his mind. I pretended to enjoy it. I suppose he did too, not that he remembered me in the morning.

I was greeted with a How did you get in here? to which I replied by showing him all the pictures of us together that he insisted we take. Oh yeah, I m glad we took those so you ll always remember last night. Bruh! Remember it? It took almost a year for people to quit mentioning it in public. I was trying to forget it the moment he passed out on top of me.

He was kind enough to take me home in his cab, except that he told the driver the wrong address. I wasn t paying attention; I was doing my best not to tell him off for being probably one of the worst lays of my life. When we got to this place that was obviously not my home I was all but thrown out of the cab with only a Gotta get to the airport, you understand.

Luckily for me, I am nothing if not resourceful. I knew I was six blocks away from home and could identify enough landmarks to steer me in the right direction. I had gotten about a block from the house when my flip flop broke. Now I know what you re saying, and I hear you. No self-respecting gay wears flip flops, but in my defense at this time I was doing three shows a week and flip flops were the only shoes I could wear that didn t hurt my feet.

You ever have one of those nights where you and friends all need to get laid and you re having no luck at the bar so you all decide to go to sex club? No? Just me and my friends? That s cool I didn t want a shared experience with my readers any way.

I m gonna be up front with you because I feel like we ve built a trust this far into this exploration of my mind. If you re in a city that has a sex club, go. You don t have to do anything with anyone, there might be a few creepers who won t quit following you, but to be in a building surrounded by that much sexual energy is pretty cool. I will concede that while the sexual energy is cool, it does smell like cum and chlorine so be ready for that.

The way it works is, you go up to a little window, hand them your ID and twenty bucks, they hand you a locker key and a towel and then buzz you through the door. Once inside, you find your assigned locker, take all your clothes off, wrap the towel around you and the fun begins. Side note, if you are going to a sex club, wear flip flops. You will get athlete s foot walking around barefoot.

The one in Atlanta that we always went to had the lockers and private rooms on the first floor, then you d go down a flight of stairs and you were given the choice of going outside to the pool or into a dry sauna. Beyond the pool was a steam room. They also had a weight room which was always strange to me, but different strokes for different folks I guess.

I m a big fan of options and sex clubs give you just that. You could literally have sex with anyone. Is this person a third string quarter back for the local NFL team? Possibly. Is this the cop that arrested you two years ago for driving with a suspended license? Maybe.

My only issue, and this is really no one s fault but my own, is that any time I have ever been to a sex club; I had done a show earlier in the night. The problem lies in that there is usually some heavy bass EDM playing over the loud speakers and I have a bad habit of slipping into my drag walk when the beat is good. So really, that s nobody s issue but my own. I m a constant work in progress. Never stopped me from getting laid though.

Another downside is that you don t have time to properly prepare yourself for other people s kinks. I m never one to kink shame somebody, but sometimes you ve got to get in the right headspace to handle certain things.

For instance, one night a bunch of us had gone to the sex club and there was this ridiculously good looking guy that I had met in the sauna. We went back to his private room where he informed me that he wanted me to talk dirty to him while we fucked, but only wanted me to call him Dr. Seuss.

Do you know how weird it is to say out loud: Oh yeah, ride my dick, Dr. Seuss! It s a boner killer to the highest degree. I hope you are laughing at this, because it was hilarious.

I feel like I have an obligation to address the phenomenon that is Netflix and Chill.   Like who is doing this? If you ask me to come over to watch a movie, I m bringing popcorn, Little Debbie Snack Cakes, possibly some hot wings, hell, I might even grab a Hot n Ready from Lil Caesars. I ll tell you what I m not doing: shaving my balls, wearing cute underwear, or douching. If you want to put your penis in me then you should be up front and just say Come over, and let s have sex while Captain America plays in the background.   I might still bring a pizza, but that all depends on how hard you make my toes curl. Not everybody deserves a Hot n Ready   Me or the pizza.

Let me address something else that weighs heavily on my mind. If you ve been talking to a person or dating or whatever it is you crazy kids are calling it these days, and y all get to the point that sex becomes an option you owe it to that person to create a mood for the night. Ambiance is key. Light some sexy smelling candles. Get some chocolate covered fruit, but make sure you are aware of any food allergies or dietary preferences because nothing is less sexy than a trip to the ER.

Actually while we re on the topic of ER trips not being sexy, I need to share a quick story with you. There was this guy I was hooking up with once upon a time who wanted to spice things up with flavored lube. I was game even though my stance on flavored lube has always been that it makes everything twice as sticky and attracts ants. Nobody wants ants. Ants are assholes. Anyway, he tracked down some margarita flavored lube on Amazon and we ordered it. It arrives and I give it a taste. It was foul. I made it quite clear that there was no way I was putting anything with that on it in my mouth. He proceeded to pour copious amounts of this lube on my dick and started blowing me. Sometime shortly after, he starts wheezing and choking. Normally, I would ve thought these were normal blowie sounds, but something was off so I glanced down to find that his entire face was swollen. He was having an allergic reaction to one of the ingredients in the flavored lube. We didn t have sex after that.

Back to the topic at hand. Ambiance. I just really like that word. That one and bauble. Those are good words; try to work them into conversations as much as you can.

Spend some time on a sex playlist. Like *really* spend some time on it. Don t just open Spotify and search Sex Jams because you ll end up mid-coitus and The Circle of Life will start playing. True story, happened to me. I highly suggest avoiding anything by an 80s rock band or by anyone who appeared on American Idol. Clay Aiken has never recorded any music that could be remotely considered sexy and that my friend is a fact!

My Sexy Time Playlist
1. Untitled (How Does It Feel) by D Angelo
2. This Woman s Work by Maxwell
3. Red Light Special by TLC
4. Pillowtalk by Zayn Malik
5. Rope Burn by Janet Jackson
6. Earned It by The Weekend
7. You re Makin Me High by Toni Braxton
8. By Your Side by Sade
9. Rock the Boat by Aaliyah
10. I ll Make Love to You by Boyz II Men
11. Giving Him Something He Can Feel by En Vogue
12. Weak by SWV
13. No Ordinary Love by Sade
14. All the Man that I Need by Whitney Houston
15. Lately by Divine
16. So Anxious by Ginuwine
17. If I Ever Fall in Love by Shai
18. Why by Annie Lennox
19. Purple Rain by Prince
20. Crown Royal by Jill Scott

Are these songs guaranteed to work for you? Not at all. These are the songs that I use and that work for me. Use music that makes you feel sexy and want to do sexy things. For the love of all that is good in the world don t pick something from a Disney film. Nothing about a Disney film is sexy.

I really need someone to explain the appeal of cottaging to me. Cottaging is the practice of cruising for sex in a public restroom, mostly a gay thing. If it s the thrill that you might get caught, ok, I ve pretty much got the gist of why it s done. Otherwise, I m gonna take a hard pass on that one. I ve never been in a public restroom and been like: Y know what? I d like to railed in this stall. Y all lost your fucking minds when Britney Spears was pictured leaving a gas station bathroom barefoot and you re out here fucking in them? Again, if this is your thing you do you boo.

I m not saying that I ve never had sex in a public place because, as we have already talked about, I have. Not to mention that there was one time I had sex on the hood of a Ford Explorer outside a gay bar in Birmingham   In full view of everyone on the patio, but that s neither here nor there.

And then there s figging.   This absolutely blows my mind. Figging is the practice of putting a piece of skinned ginger into the anus or vagina of another person, usually as a form of punishment. Ok, first of all, ginger is god damn expensive so, no, it s not going in my ass. Secondly, do you know what a pain it is to peel ginger? Is that the punishment part?   You ve been very naughty, as punishment you will peel this whole ginger root and then I will insert it into your anus!   Hard pass. Perhaps we could stop by the local grocery and pick up some ginger root extract? Couple of drops will have the same effect and we will have saved forty-eight hours of me standing in the kitchen trying to peel ginger with a dull tea spoon.

Legitimate question for people with pets. What do you do with them when you re gonna have sex? Because, like, my dog basically has the run of the house. He sleeps in my bed, is allowed to get on the couch, orders pay-per-view, so locking him out of the bedroom is not an option unless I want to come out to find him pissing in the kitchen sink.

On the flip side of that, you *obviously* can t have your pets in the room while you re getting down to business. Things start to get a little intense and next thing you know Fido is licking your taint or your cat starts nibbling on your toes. Even if they don t suddenly become active participants, they just sit there and watch, looking all judgmental and shit. Finished already, Dad? That was disappointing even by my standards. I m open to suggestions really.

By this point you re probably thinking that I have never had good sex. That s not entirely true. Everything that I ve mentioned here are the funny stories. While good sex can be funny, those moments I like to hold close to the vest. Those are special memories that I ll probably share another time.

Buy Your Own Fucking Plates

I won t say that I hate weddings, because that would be untrue. I m down for any over the top celebration. I m a huge fan of awards shows and a wedding is a kind of award show for two people in love. Just a big ignorant party for two people who fell in love.

That being said, I am a terrible wedding guest. I m not here to celebrate your love, I m here for the free food and, if you love your guests, the open bar. I might also be here to be the only white person who can correctly do the electric slide.

I applaud any two people who can stand in front of all their friends and family, sometimes in a church, and lie through their teeth. I mean really, you promise not to dwell on the little things that they do that sometimes irritate you? Oh and they promise not to watch *Scandal* without you? Lies. You ve both already done those things *today*! You expect me to believe you re not going to do them for the rest of your time on earth? Lies.

A tip from a constant wedding guest: Your ceremony should not last longer than about twenty to twenty-five minutes. After that we re bored, fidgety, and your great-aunt Helen s hemorrhoids are starting to flare. There s no need to write your own vows, have your second cousin who once auditioned to be Jodi Whatley s backup singer to sing something, or for there to be readings of any kind. You can do these things at the reception when your guests are good and liquored up. We will be far more appreciative of your second cousin s doo wop rendition of His Eye is on the Sparrow.

Also, don t half-ass a theme wedding. If you re gonna have a themed wedding, you better go *all the way in*. If *Star Wars* is your thing, I want Chewbacca officiating the ceremony. *Harry Potter* fan? An owl better drop off my fucking invitation. Civil War buff? Well   Just avoid this one. It s racist and gross. It s probably best to avoid any and all period themed weddings. Nobody likes those.

We need to talk about wedding registries. If you are a sensible person, you ve obviously done the smart thing and lived with the person you are about to marry. That being said; why didn t y all go to Bed, Bath, & Beyond to get stuff for your house then instead of waiting until you got engaged? Surely you needed a flatware set before now. Why are you registering for coat hangers? And not even the good ones! Some of y all are registering for the cheap plastic ones that cost fourteen cents for ninety.

I had a friend who opted not to register for actual gifts, but instead wanted guests to give the couple money that would go towards their honeymoon. When I got the invitation, I gave him a call.

Friend: Hey man, what s up?
Me: Oh nothing, just got your wedding invitation with the note about the honeymoon donations.
Friend: Yeah? Good idea, right? It was--
Me: HAHAHAHAHAHAHAHAHAHAHA No. *Click*

Look, if I m paying money for a trip, then I m going on that trip. Like I m not paying for you and your sweetheart to go to Barbados to possibly party it up with Rihanna. I ll slip you a tenner at the reception for a pack of condoms or some good lube. I m kidding, you can t buy good lube for ten bucks.

I ve seen some outright ridiculous wedding registries. I know a couple who registered at IKEA. Bitch, that s furniture! I m not buying you a couch! Did you really register for kitchen cabinets? Really? They got meatballs and a fake bamboo plant.

Quit enabling these greedy ass newly-weds by buying expensive shit from their registry. It s all a mind game. They like to see who loves them the most. Nobody needs Michael Kors bedding, couples just want to see if anybody is actually gonna buy that shit. Who needs place settings for sixty people? You don t have that many friends. I know you in real life!

Why are some of y all including your pets in your wedding ceremony? That s the dumbest shit I ve seen in a long time. I don t need your bulldog, running down the aisle, with a pillow strapped to its back only to drop a turd about midway there. There s nothing cute about that.

Speaking of not cute, please find a caterer who offers more dinner options than just: beef, chicken, or vegetarian. In my experience with catered wedding receptions, the beef is always a funny color, the chicken is dry, and the vegetarian option is always some sad excuse for a salad. You always have to go out afterwards and grab a burger because wedding food is never filling.

You know what I really appreciate these days about technology and weddings? That now there are people who are livestreaming their wedding. GOD BLESS WHOEVER CAME UP WITH THIS IDEA! If I can celebrate your love from the comfort of my living room wearing only my underwear or re-watch it on my lunch break because I couldn t get the day off from work, you really are a true friend.

Livestreaming your wedding is also good for me because every wedding I ve ever been to has been videoed and I have chronic stank face. I can t help it. I could be having the best time in the world and still look like I just smelled a fart. People making wedding videos love to zoom in on my face during especially tender moments. Everybody else is crying or smiling or both and I m just sat there looking mildly put out by the whole business; which will then lead to your new spouse wanting to know why I look mad about your whole wedding ceremony. This will open a whole can of worms for you because it ll now look like I m the side piece that you invited to your wedding.

You know what? Just don t invite me to your wedding. It s best for everybody if I sit this one out. I ll come to the next one.

Your #MCM Ate My Ass

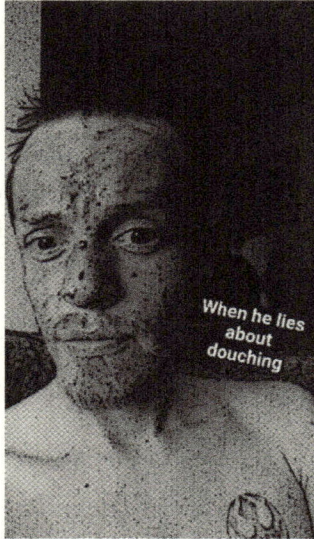

When he lies about douching

If we re dating then I m for you one hundred and twelve percent.
I m the type that will text you nine million times a day, tag you in all
that cute shit on Facebook, Snapchat you pictures of my asshole at
random intervals, you know all the things you do to keep a
relationship fresh and exciting.

My relationship history is a lot like that scene from *Final
Destination 2* where the logs fall off that truck and kill everybody,
it s a lot like that except nobody has died   Yet. I m not going to sit
here and act like I m completely innocent in the demise of just about
every relationship I ve ever had, because I m not. I ve done some
fucked up stuff to some really good guys. I ve cheated, I ve ghosted,
and I broke up with a guy through e-mail on Myspace once. If I ve
said it once I ve said it a thousand times, I am quite literally the
worst.

There was this one actor in Atlanta that I dated for like a hot minute.
He looked like every illustration of a Hobbit ever. Short, kinda
smashed in face, adorable in that way that you love a puppy that was
thrown out of a moving vehicle. He was in a couple episodes of *One*

Tree Hill back in the day. I always watch for him when I binge the show because he was fat and it makes me feel good about myself for the 2.5 seconds that he s on the screen. We broke up because I texted him twice in one day. No, really. It happened. I texted him once to say good morning and then again later in the day to just see how things were going for him. I don t know about y all, but I appreciate the hell out of shit like that. Oh, you took time out of your day to check on me? You re getting your dick sucked next time I see you.

After he ended things, he used to bring dates into the pizza place that I worked. This became a recurring trend for him until I put a whole wet mop head on his pizza and dropped it off at the table. Don t fuck with the people who handle your food.

There was one guy, Luke, who I met right after I moved to Atlanta. He was fucking perfect in every way. He liked the same booze that I liked, he was always down for me to text him, hated cuddling. Said romantic shit like: You look beautiful in this light, and Damn, your dick tastes good. All the things that make you wanna marry somebody. I lost touch with him up until he moved out to Los Angeles. Around this same time I was becoming immersed in Atlanta s drag scene and basically lost touch with everyone. We re friends on Facebook now so I can keep up with how he s doing. He s a sweetheart and I miss spending time with him.

I guess the only reason I mention those two instances is for frame of reference. It gives you an idea of how my love life can go from one extreme to another. It s a vicious cycle. I date one guy who treats me like absolute garbage then I go on to date another guy who is perfect for me, but I end up pulling the plug because I feel like something else is more important.

One of the great loves of my life. Also, I am very drunk in this picture.

By the time my parents were my age they had three kids and had been married for a while. I used to think that there was something wrong with me because I hadn t followed that same timeline. Then I would see people I went to high school with who are already on their second marriage and realize that maybe I had had the right idea of not rushing into things.

I m not judging those people I went to high school with. They re all mostly straight and had readily available options. I, however, had more life to live before I settled down. Sex, drugs, rock & roll and all that jazz.

My biggest pet peeve of relationships and people in general, is that some of y all love to air your dirty laundry all over social media. Nobody cares that your husband said you had cankles, Linda. That s private. Hilarious, but private. Nobody on Facebook cares except the people that hate you and you shouldn t even be friends with those kinds of people. You don t need that kind of negativity and dry ass macaroni in your life.

Also, on the subject of relationships, why are some of y all still obsessed with your ex? That shit is over and done with move on! They re not occupying their time worried about whose genitals you re putting in your mouth so don t be worried about them. You can be friends with your ex all day long and up a dog s ass, but only if it s a healthy friendship. If y all broke up because of some toxic shit, yours or theirs, remove them from your life. Neither of you needs that.

It has taken me a long time to realize that when it comes to love and being happy there s no real timeline. There s no guidebook, there s no right or wrong way to do it. There s somebody out there for everyone and they ll find you eventually. In the meantime, though? Keep sucking dicks, write a book, have your cake and eat it to, do what makes you happy and stop worrying about finding a significant other, your time will come.

Yes, All Men

As a man I have no problem saying that, yes, all men are garbage. Even more certainly than that, I can say that without a doubt all white men are garbage.

White men hold all the power in this country and use it to keep anyone they feel is a threat (namely people of color, women, and anyone who doesn t subscribe to the gender binary) one rung lower than them on the ladder of success.

I m sure there are a number of men reading this book who will find any reason to exclude themselves from what I m saying.   But I m gay!   Garbage.   I m one sixteenth Cherokee!   Nope, still garbage. Gay men are still men and you re supposed First Nations ancestry is a lie you tell yourself to feel better for the fact that white people raped and stole their way to control over this country.

It s baffling to me that white people are the first ones to say that there s no room for refugees in the United States when we ourselves were refugees who came here. There are a number of viral Facebook videos of a Linda or Karen freaking the hell out because someone who immigrated to this country is speaking their native language in a Starbucks. Have a seat, Helen! If speaking the language of America was so god damn important to you we would be speaking one of the First Nations languages right now.

What white people fear more than anything else is becoming a minority in this country. This fear is prevalent because we re afraid that we ll be treated the same way we ve treated minorities in the past. If you need proof of this, just look at any of the social media posts made by your not-so-secretly racist relatives during the presidency of Barack Obama. For eight years, he was called the n-slur, a terrorist and any other racist thing you can think of. Was Obama an infallible president? Good lord, no, but he handled a lot being thrown at him and he handled it well.

Gentlemen, while I have you absolutely fuming, there is nothing

funny about rape. Rape is not the victim s fault   *EVER*. It doesn t
matter what they were wearing, if they had been drinking, or where
they were. If they did not consent to having sex with your gross ass
it is rape and you are trash.

The supposed friend zone is not a real thing. A person does not
have to want your dick to be your friend. You are not owed sex.
Say that with me: *I am not owed sex*.

Also, let s clear up another common misconception. Consensual
sex is just sex, it doesn t need a modifier. Nonconsensual sex is
rape. There s sex and there is rape. Rape is never ok.

We, as men, have got to start having tough conversations with our
 bros if we are ever going to make women and gender
nonconforming people feel safe around us. If one of your friends or
relatives makes a sexist joke, you ve got to call him out for that. If
race, gender, religion, or sexual identity has to be the punchline, it s
not a joke it s hate speech.

If a sex worker is raped, it is still rape. It does not come with job
like long hours at a factory or a constant headache from having to
deal with your gross ass. Sex work is *actual* work. It is a job just
like your nine-to-five that you go to every day, five days a week.
Confused about what sex work is? Just like your job, they are
exchanging services, usually of a sexual nature, for money. A sex
worker could include, but is not limited to escorts, exotic dancers,
and many other professions of a sexual nature. It s amazing to me
that Heidi Fleiss went to jail for *running a business*. This falls to the
fact that men are afraid of sexuality. Men are especially afraid of a
person who owns their sexuality and uses it to make money.

Just like with the topic of making women and gender nonconforming
people feel safe around men, we also have to start having the tough
talks about racism. If you have ever said or thought that you
wouldn t do XYZ with a person of color because of their race, you
are a racist. I ve addressed this briefly in regards to hookup apps,
but this goes for everyday life as well. I worked with someone who
once said that if they couldn t pronounce the name on the application

they wouldn t hire them. No, really, that happened and I had to tell this person that their hiring practices were racist. It was awkward and made me uncomfortable, but that s how you know that it s the right thing to do.

If having conversations about racism makes you uncomfortable, good. It means you re unlearning racist behavior. Just like when your non-black friend is rapping along to a song that contains the n-word, if they say it too then you need to have a conversation with that friend. The n-word is not for non-black people. Just like fag is not for non-gay people.

I guess really what I don t understand is how when people of color tell a white person that something is racist said white person flies off the handle instead of apologizing and trying to do better.

White people need to do better. Unlearning racist behaviors is going to be tough, but we can do it.

I'll Probably Get Sued for This

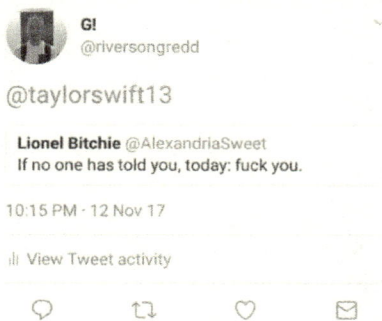

Follow me on the Twitter!

I keep a list of celebrities that I would fight if I ever saw them on the
street. hey run the gamut of various forms of entertainment.
Stephen Hawking is on the list just to give you an idea of how vast
my pool of famous people I hate actually is.

Here are some of the highlights:

Taylor Swift
Taylor Swift is the worst. Like literally, the worst. Every time she
speaks or descends from her ivory tower of white feminism I get
irrationally angry. I think it s the fact that every word that comes out
of her mouth is a lie. That she vilified Kanye West for the better part
of her career and has milked every relationship. She built a career
out of being the victim until Kim Queen of Receipts Kardashian
put a stop to all that nonsense. Let s not forget that this is also a
person who sued fans who made tribute videos and merchandise.
That s totally true, Google it. I hate Taylor for moral reasons and
also because I liked *1989* which caused me great emotional distress.
Odds of Winning: 2/1

Tyra Banks
I had a dream once that Tyra Banks murdered my hamster when I
was kid and since then it has been no secret that she is my arch
nemesis. Let s put it this way: I hate Tyra Banks the way that Tyra

Banks thinks that Naomi Campbell hates her in that the feud doesn t actually exist because Tyra doesn t know who I am in the same way that Naomi Campbell has no idea who Tyra Banks is. Also, Top Model was garbage after season 3.
Odds of Winning: 6/1

Paul Hollywood
If you don t automatically recognize his name then you are not familiar with the glorious show that is *The Great British Bake Off*. It used air on BBC1 before some tricky negotiations that ended with a move to E4 and a shakeup of the hosts and judges. The two hosts and one judge left the show because they didn t feel the show would hold the same magic on E4 that it had on the BBC. Paul Hollywood stayed on. Fuck you, Paul Hollywood.
Odds of Winning: 15/1

The Whos of Whoville
Yes, the Christmas loving Whos of Whoville made the list. I won t ever get the opportunity to fight one, unless I go to a Christmas parade and there some unfortunate soul dressed as one and then its clobberin time. But really, the Whos are problematic as fuck. Racist ass Dr. Seuss characters persecuting the Grinch because he was green and broody. No wonder he stole your Christmas.
Odds of Winning: 0/1

Carson Daly
He s a douche. Full stop.
Odds of Winning: 3/1

Cameron Diaz
My distaste for Cameron Diaz stems from the fact that she broke Justin Timberlake s heart. That and she calls herself an actress. Insert Marcia Brady Sure Jan gif here. The last good movie that Cameron Diaz made was *Charlie's Angels* and we all know that Lucy Liu carried that movie. She s not even that cute.
Odds of Winning: 1/1

Jimmy Fallon
THERE IS NOTHING FUNNY ABOUT JIMMY FALLON! He

was, by far, the weakest host of Weekend Update on SNL and he ruined every sketch he was ever in. Also, he stole the *Tonight Show* hosting gig from Conan O Brien.
Odds of Winning: 6/1

The guy who decided that gif was pronounced like jif
Fuck that guy! No part of your decision makes any sense.
Odds of Winning: 1/1

That isn t even the full list, just some of the standouts. The imaginary fights that I would have a chance in hell of actually winning because I am not a fighter. Like the title states I m probably going to get sued for this, but at least I ll have an interesting story to tell my non-existent grandchildren while I m in prison. Do people go to prison for libel or is it something that you just have to pay a settlement for and stay at least one thousand feet away from the petitioner? Much like how many licks it takes to get to the center of a tootsie pop, the world may never know. Someone in the world probably does know, it s one of those things that I could Google, but it s 11:50 PM and I m really forcing myself to write this chapter.

You are free to call me a crazy person for having a list of celebrities I d like to assault. I know this behavior is not normal. It s just another one of those things that makes my parents embarrassed to be seen in public with me. I like to think that they are afraid that I might have to dropkick Cameron Diaz and they ll be forced to apologize profusely while the police cart me away.

I have a mild obsession with celebrity culture. I love to flip through *National Enquirer* or *News of the World* while I m standing in the checkout line. Wait! What kind of store am I at that doesn t have self-checkout? What year is this?

I don t fuck with the Kardashians though. Just not my cup of tea. I am going to talk about them shortly, though.

I think about random shit when it comes to the offspring of celebrities too. Like, will Apple Martin and Shiloh Jolie-Pitt be allowed to date? How long until Blue Ivy actually takes over the world? Are Bear Payne and Freddie Tomlinson going to become Wham 2.0? Will Jaden Smith run for president one day? These are the things that keep me up at night.

Tumblr is a good place to get good celebrity info. It s is also a good place to find free porn, but that s neither here nor there. Celebrity Stans run rampant on Tumblr man. TMZ should pay those kids. They are waiting outside studios, restaurants, public restrooms. They can tell you what they have on that day, what label it is, where you too can purchase it. It s both frightening and intriguing all at once.

Be careful though, click one too many times and you ll end up in a k-hole of slash truthers that will have you watching a six hour YouTube video on proof that two celebrities are dating on the low. One night, I fucked around and was entirely convinced that Zayn Malik and Liam Payne were married and that the government of Bolivia was keeping it under wraps. I mean, I m still not completely convinced they AREN T married. Maybe I m just gullible.

Also, while I m thinking about it, why are celebrities still sending dick pics and jerk off videos to random people on Snapchat? It s 2017! At least it is right now. You ve gotta have better sense. You send a dirty snap and suddenly all your naughty bits are gonna be all over the internet. You can t trust anybody.

That is, of course, unless your name is Tyler Posey and then you release your own dirty Snapchat video to stand in solidarity with one of your cast mates whose nudes were leaked. I don t buy that, but whatever floats his boat. Tyler Posey is one of those celebrities that wants to be gay so bad, but was not blessed with the hardwiring to take a dick or four. They want to be gay in the same way that Eminem wants to be black without actually have to *be* black. All the street cred, but none of the persecution. It s gross.

As I sit here writing this, I m trying to put my finger on the exact moment that Gwenyth Paltrow lost her damn mind and started that *GOOP* bullshit. Probably when she married Coldplay. Yes, I know Coldplay is a band and not a person, but could you recognize any of the other members on the street? Didn t think so. It s like U2 is made up of those two guys and who? Nobody else.

GOOP touts itself as a carefully curated lifestyle magazine, it s like Gwenyth s answer to *O Magazine*, but complete horse shit. If you ve ever heard or read anything about it you know that it s wild. There s an article on the site right now about bathing in dew. The moisture that s on the grass in the morning. Bathing in that. Like, who is gonna collect that shit for you? Who has time for that? Gwenyth, girl, get your life together. You and Apple need to go to McDonald s. I m worried for you. Are you a Scientologist? Are you in danger? Blink twice for yes.

I d really like to know what Kris Jenner has on Ryan Seacrest and the good folks over at E! What does she know that warrants those ninety-seven hours of programming a day, sixteen spinoffs, and a twelve hour long Christmas special? No one is interesting enough to warrant that amount of television, not even that family. At the height of her popularity, Paris Hilton didn t even saturate the market that much. I will give it to them that they have done extremely well at branding themselves as America s favorite train wrecks, but there s only so many times I can watch those girls sit around picking at salads bitching at each other for not returning phone calls or for borrowing a Fendi bag that they didn t even pay for!

Even more important, I m not entirely convinced that Kim *isn't* holding Kanye hostage in their Calabasas home.

My favorite Kardashian moments are the random times when Beyoncé and Kim are in the same room and Kim acts like Bey is her BFF and Beyoncé just looks absolutely horrified that Kim would dare breathe the same oxygen as her. Really any time anyone who is legitimately talented and famous is around a Kardashian I love to see the disgust on their faces.

Kourtney is the only member of that family with a lick of damn sense in her head. She married a nobody, turned him into a monster that no one wanted to be around, had two kids, and then divorced him. Clever girl.

I used to think that Rob Kardashian was really cute. I mean he still kind of is, in the face. But, like, when did he turn into a reclusive Larry Flint? I get it now, because we all thought he was gonna turn his life around when he shacked up with Blac Chyna, but she played his ass all the way to the bank. God, I love her.

Speaking of people with no business being famous. Why is Gigi Hadid the more famous of the Hadid sisters? Because she s fucking Zayn Malik? It surely can t be because she s a model, because she walks like she has a prolapsed rectum. Bella Hadid is more *model* pretty. She doesn t look like she walked off an American Eagle ad campaign. Bella s features are more interesting. She s odd looking in the Isabella Rossellini/Helena Bonham Carter way. Gigi is a clothes hanger, Bella *wears* clothes.

That s really what I miss about the first few seasons of ANTM. In the first like three or four seasons, none of the contestants was conventionally pretty. There was something slightly off about all the girls looks. They were interesting to look at. Not to mention that the meltdowns during the makeover episodes were absolute madness and made for great TV. Now, she s putting a weave beard on one dude and letting Rita Ora host the VH1 reboot. How are you gonna reboot a show that just went off the air fifteen minutes ago?

In all honesty, I really need for Hollywood to chill with all the reboots and sequels. Not everything needs to be redone. There was no need for Fantastic Four reboot. The first films only redeeming qualities were that Chris Evans took his shirt off every three minutes. We didn t care the first time and we re certainly not going to care this time. Especially when Michael B. Jordan stays dressed for the majority of the film. The X-Men reboots are really the ones I ll stand behind because they were remade with better stories and a better cast.

Why are there *three* Pitch Perfect movies? *WHY?* There were not more stories that needed be told there. Let the first one be a cute stand-alone film that under-utilized it s only queer character of color and let s move on with our lives. Like it s amazing to me that we can have three Pitch Perfect films shoved down our throats but I can t get a sequel to *The Labyrinth*. Get your shit together Hollywood. Listen to the voice of the people! Not me, obviously, because I would pay good money for a *Love Actually* sequel, but y know someone who knows what they re talking about.

While we re on the topic of reboots and sequels that need to stop happening: I need for American television to stop trying to make versions popular British television shows. The only time that has been remotely successful has been with *The Office*. All the others have failed miserably. Every Christmas ABC rolls out *The Great American Baking Show*, which is a poorly retitled version of *The Great British Bake Off*.

GBBO, as it will be known for the rest of the time I mention it, is amazing because it takes all the things that you know about cooking competitions and throws them out the window. In other cooking competitions they give you like twenty minutes to cook a forty course meal for nine million people. On *GBBO*, they give you seventy-two hours to make two cupcakes. It s very relaxing to watch and you get a chance to *really* get to know the contestants to the point that you even root for the guy who fucked up a dacquoise. A dacquoise is a cake made up of layers of finely chopped almonds and meringue usually topped with buttercream or whipped cream. Who fucks up a dacquoise? I mean really, dude, get your shit together.

Andrew Cunanan Did Not Want to Kill Me Too...
Probably

On 15 July 1997 Gianni Versace was murdered by a former fling by the name of Andrew Cunanan. Coverage of the nationwide manhunt for Cunanan was *everywhere*. Any time you turned on the TV somebody was talking about where he had been seen or who his next victim might possibly be.

I was 14 at the time and was completely convinced that Andrew Cunanan wanted to murder me too. I was borderline paranoid that this dude who had no idea who I was or that I even existed was going to gun me down in my home.

The thing was I had watched just as much, if not more, coverage of the OJ Simpson trial and did not think for half a second that The Juice was going to kill me. That s probably because I thought he was innocent and did so enjoy him in the Naked Gun movies.

I never voiced my concern about the possibility of my impending death, I just double and triple checked all the locks on our doors and then went back to watching more news coverage of the manhunt. I used to walk to school around this time, usually by myself, which made it all the more frightening. I used to act like I was talking to someone, really loud, and obvious thinking that would scare him off.

If you haven t been able to tell by now, I am an idiot.

Andrew Cunanan killed himself on 23 July 1997 and I finally got a full night s sleep.

It s funny that tween me used to think this way and now adult me falls asleep watching *Law & Order: SVU* marathons on USA without any of the paranoia. I also think that we re so desensitized by the amount of violence in the media that if something like that happened now it wouldn t shake me.

There s no real point to this chapter. Just like my life. BOOM!
YOU RE WELCOME!

I Hate Children and Christmas
(I May Also Be the Anti-Christ)

I should probably clarify by saying that I don t *actually* hate Christmas. It s the most wonderful time of the year. It s when Michael Buble and Mariah Carey are at their most powerful. It s the only time of the year that people watch the Hallmark Channel on purpose.

I hate the inundation of everything Christmas-y that starts in October. Like I m not trying to see nativity scenes while I m out shopping for a sexy penguin costume. Relax people; Christmas will get its turn in December just like it does every year.

Is anyone else as disappointed as I am that there has never been a No Room at the Inn yard sign marketed as a Christmas decoration? Am I the only one who thinks that s funny? Yes? Damn.

I work in retail so Christmas starts for us in like August when the first glimpses of outerwear and holiday scheduling ideas first start to pop up. By the time December rolls around all retail workers are so exhausted with idea of Christmas that most don t even celebrate, it s just a paid day off. At least that s how I like to think of it.

I like Christmas music as much as the next person, but there s only so many times I can listen to the same song recorded by fifteen different people before I m contemplating arson. Carol of the Bells is my favorite Christmas song. Not every singer needs a Christmas album. Not every singer needs a career, but that s another story for another time.

You know what Christmas music I don t appreciate, though? Anything from *The Nutcracker*. I don t even like to go see the ballet production anymore. Why? Once upon a time I had to run to Wal-Mart at like 4:00 AM on Christmas. Anyone who s been to Wal-Mart in the middle of the night knows that it s super creepy, near deserted, and they turn off some of the lights so it s basically nightmare fuel. For whatever reason, they were piping the entire *Nutcracker Ballet* throughout the store. I was instantly paranoid and convinced that my life was going to end at a Wal-Mart Supercenter on December 25th.

Christmas music in general is problematic as fuck any way because you ve got songs about date rape (*Baby It's Cold Outside*) and then you ve got songs about infidelity (*I Saw Mommy Kissing Santa Claus*). Let s not even go into the fact that everyone in Rudolph the Red nose Reindeer s life was toxic as fuck and only wanted him around when he was of some use to them. *Do they know it's Christmas time at all?* No, actually, they don t. Not everyone celebrates Christmas you half-wit.

Then we have all that family togetherness. Don t get me wrong, I love my family I really do from the bottom of my heart and I m not just saying that because some of them may be reading this. I just have nothing to talk to them about for extended periods of time. Not to mention that I absolutely hate small talk so to have to explain to my fourth cousin twice removed that working retail and self-publishing a book about my life is a valid career choice for someone in their mid-thirties is not really how I d like to spend my holidays.

And while we re on the subject of families and the holidays, I want to drop a truth on you. You don t have to eat everybody s food. Not everybody can cook and you don t have to be nice to try Great Aunt Theresa s Festivus casserole because: 1) You know she doesn t wash her hands after she uses the bathroom and 2) I m not sure what Festivus casserole is because I just made it up, but it sounds gross as fuck.

And then there are the kids. Why is it that kids now act like little hellions around Christmas? When I was younger, we were scared to death of acting up because of the threat of not getting anything under the tree. Notice how I didn t say anything about Santa visiting?

Story time kids.

I haven t believed in Santa for a long *LONG* time. Since I was in kindergarten to be exact. See, there s a part in that movie *A Christmas Story*, the one with the pink bunny pajamas not the one about the Immaculate Conception and no room at the Red Roof Inn, where the parents send the kids to bed and then the dad turns to the mom and says: Let s go get the stuff. I remember watching it and going, What a god damn minute!

That film is considered a Christmas classic, but why does no one at TBS think about ruining Santa Claus for the children of the US when they air it for twenty-four hours straight on December 25th? I ll tell you why, because it is such a minute detail that unless you are paying super close attention to the film you wouldn t normally catch that little exchange. The reason I caught it? Because right after the dad says his line the film cut to a commercial and my little kindergarten brain had time to process the last scene.

My mother was devastated and being a good son, I agreed to keep the secret for the sake of my two younger brothers. I m not really sure when they stopped believing in a fat man in a red suit who has a once-a-year habit of doing a global B&E. I guess there was no big revelation or I just wasn t around for it.

So, yeah, I m just a little curious as to why kids these days are so bad. Maybe I just see things a little skewed because I hate anyone who isn t old enough to hold a full and informed discussion on the latest episode of *Game of Thrones*.

Much like my own family, I don t know how to talk to children and I certainly don t know how to talk to parents about their children. I turn into a Klingon. I m all: You have a raised a viable off-spring. They will bring great honor to your tribe.

I m just not fascinated by what they just pulled out of their noses or how much wine their Mommy drinks while she cries because Daddy is working late again. Actually, I take that back because that s the kind of stuff that I *LIVE* to hear kids talk about. Alcoholism and infidelity, now you ve got my attention Little Johnny Son-of-a-Bitch!

Also, I don t have it in me to pretend that I like a child s preschool art project. Your teacher hot glued some macaroni to a pre-cut piece of construction paper and you want me to put that on my fridge? Next to the utility bill? Where the neighbors might see it? Wrong answer kid, this is garbage and so is your career as an artist. Don t feel bad, little one, I feel the same way about Christmas cards that feature a family wearing matching sweaters and fake smiles. It s all trash.

If I ever have kids (READ: I won t), I refuse to baby talk to them. To any parents out there, please don t do this to your kids. You already look like an asshole for pushing around a tiny person who probably just shit themselves, but now you re going to make some stupid voice to try to get them to say Mama? That s the lamest party trick ever. No thanks. Not for me. If I had fallopian tubes they would ve tied themselves.

I fully admit that I baby talk my dog, but my dog is stupid and I m convinced that the only way he ll understand me is if I talk like a complete asshole. Sue me.

Parents of the world why is your toddler running around public places in only a diaper? This is a common thing that I see at my job. Put some clothes on your kid! There was one time this Linda had her baby, no more than a year or two old, walking around my store in a Pamper and some cowboy boots. Hand to God! I work in a clothing store and Linda didn t even buy anything for the baby! Just had little Joey running around looking a fool. If you re in the comfort of your own home, let the baby run naked and free as the day they were born. It s cool to not put anything on your kid if you re making a quick run through a drive-through or something, but if you go to an outdoor mall there s no reason for that little bastard to be running around in some Tony Lama s and a little SPF 100.

I don t understand this new trend among parents to dress their daughters in those weird clown outfits that are popular now. You know the one s I m talking about. The flared out pants with all the ruffles and shit on them and the top that matches. I ve even seen mothers and daughters in matching versions of these. What are y all thinking? That s not fashionable! That s Ringling Brothers, Barnum, and fucked up is what that is.

One time I saw a pre-teen girl wearing a velour sweat suit that had   Side Piece   written in glitter letters on the back of the jacket. Two things: Who let her out of the house like that? And, also, where can I get one of those?

Life with Karen

What the fuck are you typing so hard? Probably a strongly worded letter to the manager.

Classic Karen.

There are three types of white people. These are always white people that I don t know and they are the absolute worst.

Karen   Usually a woman of certain age, very career oriented, her first husband left her for his younger executive assistant, and she writes really hateful YELP reviews about local businesses. Karen can usually be found in some public space on her laptop sipping a decaf pumpkin spice latte while checking the status of her 401K. Her Facebook is almost exclusively pictures of her Siberian husky, Todd. She probably has a lesbian daughter that she doesn t speak to and voted for Donald Trump.

Linda   Mother of three, has no control of her children, always asks if there are any coupons available, refers to all white wine as Pinot Greeg , and thinks Ro-Tel is too spicy. Linda s children are all within a year of each other. Destroys retail displays because she s looking for a size. Target is her happy place. She started a Lulu Lemon business but never followed through after the initial investment now she wears the entire inventory she bought. Thinks Ugg boots are high fashion. Loves every movie that Meg Ryan has ever been in.

Helen   Professional Lifestyle blogger, claims to only shop local, but orders her groceries on Amazon, has a Starbucks order that is three minutes long, and considers the Beatles the greatest band of all time. She is an anti vaxxer even though she doesn t have any children. Knows what steal-cut oatmeal is. Claims to have a gluten intolerance, but always asks the server for extra rolls at every restaurant she goes to. Once wrote a piece for Huffington Post about Kegel exercises that wasn t very well received.

You know one, if not all, of these people. I have never taken the time to interchange male names because white men can also be Karen, Linda, or Helen. And before you tell me this isn t fair to the white women who might be reading this, just remember that 54% of white women voted for Trump. As a white person, I can say without a doubt all white people are terrible and privileged. Whether we want to admit it or not, it s a fact. White people have it super easy and if you re getting your ass chapped over a joke in a self-published book, you need to get some hobbies. Maybe start a Pinterest account or masturbate more often.

Even better, you might want to read up on the systemic racism in this country and how you can help to squash it.

Also, let me stop you before you tell me I m being racist towards white people. That s not a thing, you sound like an idiot.

Also Karen.

Fuck You and Fuck Your Coupon, Linda

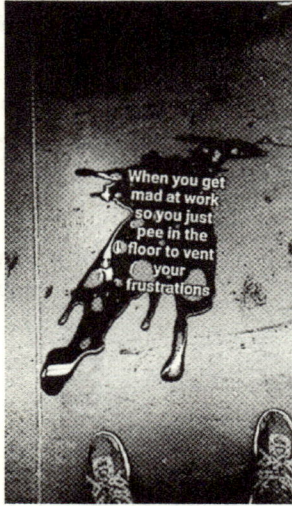

I ve had a lot of different jobs in my life. Some were great learning experiences and some were like working in the seventh circle of hell. I was a bagger at Kroger for six hours once when I was sixteen. It was the middle of the summer and they wanted me to bring the carts in from outside. It was one hundred degrees out. I left. Didn t even tell anyone, just dipped right on out.

I have worked for some really cool people though. I worked for a South African family that owned the pizza place in Atlanta. They were awesome. My current boss is the most unintentionally funny man I ve ever met.

I think my favorite person I ve ever worked for was a woman named Stephanie. She hired me to be an assistant manager at a seasonal technology store. She probably gave me the best interview I ve ever had in my entire life. It didn t even feel like a real interview, it was just two people talking about whatever in the middle of a mall. She s got a presence that commands respect and can give you a look that says: I m not having your shit right now. I could really go on for hours about her, but I won t. She taught me how to make people feel stupid without coming across as condescending and that, my friends, is the greatest lesson I ve ever learned.

I work in retail now. Retail management to be more accurate. After years in food service, I wanted to switch things up and being some sort of masochist I figured why not try retail. Retail is hell. I thought people were crazy when they went out to eat, baby let me tell you, people are absolutely wild when it comes to their clothing.

Before anyone says Well, no one is forcing you to do it! Let me just tell you something, you should be nice to the people who work retail because without us, who would help you find that size sixteen husky for your jackass son who has a lollipop stuck to the side of his head? Who I ask you? WHO?

I don t know why, but there are people in this world who absolutely lose their minds while shopping for clothes and then act like it s a huge inconvenience that they can t find the size they are looking for on a table that they just tore apart. Retail people get more irritated when you fuck up what we were just working than if you had just asked for help. I work somewhere on the lower end of brand name retail, it s a recognizable name that you probably have one or two pieces from. As this is my first book, I won t say the actually name of where I work because I want to keep my job. Plus I don t know y all like that; I don t want you showing up to my job.

Things That Have Been Said to Me by Customers and My Imaginary Responses:

  Where is your in-house tailor?
This is not Neiman's, please leave.

  Wouldn t it be great if there were a size between a small and a large?
That's a medium. Please leave.

  I bought this at *insert the name of literally any other store* can I return it here?
Please leave.

If it doesn t ring up it must be free!
You're not funny, Karen. Please leave.

I can get it cheaper at *insert the name of literally any other store*!
Please leave.

I got a shirt here forty years ago, do y all still have that?
You're an idiot. Please leave.

Has Google open on their phone What time do y all close?
Please leave.

I m going on a mission trip and I ll be back in like three months. Can I put this on hold until I come back?
Please leave.

I know you re closing in forty-five seconds, but I m just gonna try on 100 pairs of jeans.
Fuck you. Please leave.

Calls the store Are y all open?
Stay home.

Is actively destroying a table that I just folded. Looks me dead in my face. This place is always such a mess!
I hope you choke on a dick. Please leave.

One of my favorite customer interactions has to be the time that I asked an older gentleman if he needed help finding anything and he looked me right in the eye and replied: What do you care? He was not wrong, I don t really care I get paid to pretend I do though so just bear with me.

My store has these shopping carts that Lindas love to leave just sitting wherever, usually in the middle of Christ and everything, while they go look around in other parts of the store. Then they get all pissy when one of my associates empties the cart. Don t leave shit that you intend to buy while you go look somewhere else otherwise it s getting put away, I ve gotta keep this house clean.

While we re on the subject, my store provides benches for people to sit on while trying on shoes or while you re waiting for someone in the fitting room. Please explain to me why you are sitting on a table on top of a stack of freshly folded shirts? And why, exactly, are you trying on those sneakers while sitting the middle of Christ and everything in one of the main walkways? You re in my way, and you *know* you re in my way so why did you sit down there in the first place?

Also, why are y all leaving your keys and your phones just lying around? Every day there are at least four people who have set their phone, keys, or some other personal item on a table to look for something and then just walked off without it. Are you a goldfish? Do you have no memory? Keep up with your shit! And should you for some odd reason actually lose something, don t ask me to help you find it. You lost it, you find it, I ve got things to do. I have to go pretend to be busy in a part of the store that you are not in.

Once this man lost his keys and was in my store with mall security looking for them and the security guard had the audacity to ask me to help them look for this dude s keys. Nah, man, your stupid ass fell for that sob story, I m not helping y all.

I m the type of person that if you say something stupid, it will read all over my face, so I try to avoid interaction with stupidity as much as possible. I usually fail.

My favorite thing that customers try to pull is when they say that our signs are misleading. What s misleading about the sign? It s says UP TO 60% OFF . It s not my fault that your reading comprehension skills didn t survive past middle school. No, I m not going to discount your items because you misread the sign. No ma am, quite frankly, I don t care if you never shop here again. Yes, you can absolutely speak to my supervisor, they re going to tell you the same thing I did. Oh, you want the corporate number?

Awesome, you can be someone else s problem. Next customer, please.

Retail employees do not care about your life story. If you ask us to help you find something, keep it short and to the point. We don t need the whole backstory about how your daughter s best friend s niece is getting married and they asked your son to be an usher and you just *have* to find the perfect pair of slacks for him to wear. Who the fuck says slacks anyway? Bitch, they re pants Or trousers if you re in the United Kingdom.

And while I m thinking about it, please stop trying hats on in a store. Do you want lice? That s how you get lice. You don t know whose head that hat has been on! Common sense, people.

If you ve made it this far into the book, you know that I m not exactly the most family-friendly person. In a sheer twist of fate, I am what is basically equal to Human Resources at any other business. No, you really did read that right. I should basically wear a shirt that says NSFW. I m terribly inappropriate for someone who is supposed to make sure that everyone follows the rules.

It s hard to be in management, especially in a position like mine, because you want to be someone your employees feel like they can talk to, but at the same time you want to shake them and ask if they are really that stupid.

I would love my job a lot more if there were no people involved. Maybe that s why I ve taken to writing because I don t have to deal with anyone else, just me, the computer, and millions of people online who could potentially hate this book. Fuck!

Who is Casting Winona Ryder in Period Pieces?

I like to have some kind of background noise while I write.
Sometimes music, sometimes a movie, sometimes whatever happens
to be on TV at the moment.

I have since learned that while writing you should absolutely *NOT*
have anything with words playing in the background   Oops.

Today, *Little Women* is on. The 1994 version starring Winona
Ryder, Susan Sarandon, and a host of other 90s powerhouse
actors. The one where Claire Danes character gets scarlet fever and
in real life, too. As I sit here with my back to the television, I m
acutely more aware of the voices than I would be if I were sitting on
the couch.

It makes me wonder who had the idea to cast Winona Ryder in any
period pieces. I know she was a big deal up until she was arrested
for shoplifting, but my god at what cost? She did a string of period
movies in the 90s from *Bram Stoker's Dracula* to *Little Women* to
The Crucible and, of course, today s selection *Little Women*.

Her accent is so affected that it is almost jarring. Surely after the
first period movie, someone somewhere was like Yeah, we
probably shouldn t cast her in any film that takes place prior to
1970.

There was actually a cut-away gag from *Family Guy* several years
back that referenced this, but it s not something that I ever really and
truly thought about until today. It s bad y all!

On the flipside of this, why does Susan Sarandon always sound like
she s acting in a period film?

They ll probably cast Winona Ryder to play me in the movie about
my life. Don t let this happen.

Anyway, Here's Wonderwall...

The year is 2002. *American Idol* has just wrapped their groundbreaking first season with Kelly Clarkson as their inaugural winner.

It became your basic watercooler fodder. Everybody had an opinion, a favorite, and the time on their hands to vote a million and twelve times.

Shortly thereafter auditions for season 2 were announced. I was a theater gay in high school, reckoned that I was marginally talented, so I figured why the fuck not.

So on 29 October 2002, I hopped in my 1989 Plymouth Grand Voyager and headed to Nashville. I got to Nashville, checked into my hotel, and went to scout the audition venue. The first round of auditions this particular year were being held at the Ryman Auditorium.

There were already several thousand people in line when I cruised by, so I went back to the hotel, dropped my van off, and walked the three blocks back to the Ryman to get in line. What you don t see on TV when they show those sweeping shots of all the *Idol* hopefuls is that those poor people have slept outside the audition venue. They probably haven t showered, and generally are not in a great mood.

In the particular instance of when I auditioned, it was October in Nashville so during the day it was lovely weather, but as soon as the sun set we were all freezing our nips off. Of course, the serious musicians in the group had their scarves on since they woke up two weeks ago and took to sipping hot tea as soon as temperatures began to drop. You could spot the people who took themselves too seriously because they looked exactly like what you think hipsters look like now.

Given the close proximity you couldn t help but form little cliques. I don t want to say friendships because I didn t speak to any of the people around me after those thirty-six hours in line. We were friendly out of necessity not because we wanted to be. In the my clique was a girl from Kentucky whose father was in prison for selling meth or maybe it was racketeering; The son of some guy who owned a chain of White Castles in West Virginia who if this doesn t pan out my dad is gonna back my studio album ; a guy who swore he was the second coming of Anastacia and me. We could have been the off off off off Broadway cast of Rent that was performed in a 75th Street laundromat.

After literally thirty-six hours outside we re herded into the Ryman auditorium like immigrants coming into Ellis Island for the first time. You then had to wait in line *again* to get your contestant number. Once all that was out of the way, you just had to wait until they called your group of numbers.

At this point lots of things happened. First, there were fights over bathrooms because you didn t dare get out of line even to pee. And let s face when you re under twenty-one and in downtown Nashville at 4 AM your options for bathrooms are severely limited. Secondly, the people that you just spent the night with, who not even ten minutes ago, were extremely disheveled now looked like they had just stepped out of an Abercrombie & Fitch Ad. The family friendly ones, not the softcore porn quarterlies that you had to be eighteen to buy in stores. We re talking full makeup and hair at 9 o clock in the morning.

I had none of that going for me. I was in a hoodie and a pair of jeans, hadn t slept the night before because I was terrified of getting kidnapped by Al Qaeda. No, really, this was a valid concern because American Idol had become such a hit that people, myself included, thought that there would be terrorist attacks at the auditions. You also have to keep in mind, the 9/11 terror attacks were just over a year before this happened so the country was a little on edge.

Another fun thing that happened during the second or third waiting period was that they parade Ryan Seacrest around like a show pony. I have no love for Ryan Seacrest and I make that no secret. If you watch videos of the season two auditions, there s a part during the Nashville auditions where Seacrest is talking to the cameras and you can see me in the background rolling my eyes.

This was the early days of Idol so a lot of people who were auditioning didn t know that you auditioned for producers before you actually got to audition in front of Randy, Paula, and Simon. Maybe some people knew that, I was not one of those people. What I did know was that I could totally pass the background check and full psych evaluation that was coming my way if I was gonna make it to Hollywood.

I waited for around an hour in the Ryman s main room that was covered in hay, so I assume there was some kind of rodeo or barnyard animal related event sometime before the auditions. They called my group of numbers and we followed someone s assistant down to a conference room where a balding man with a really unfortunate mullet sat behind a folding table.

There was a line taped on the floor to one side of him and an X taped on the floor directly in front of him. We were instructed to stand along the tape line and when our number was called to step up to the X and sing our audition song.

My number was called third. I was terrified, exhausted, a little smelly, hungry, and was just starting to realize that maybe this was a mistake. I did think I had one ace in the hole though. My audition song. I was sure that this guy would be surprised by my choice to sing *Miss Celie's Blues* from *The Color Purple*.

I step up to the little X on the floor. Upon closer inspection I m realizing that maybe it s a T .

Whenever you re ready, mullet guy says to me. I almost feel bad for him because I wonder if he was kind of a big deal in the 90s and now he s relegated to working as a grunt producer on *American Idol* now. I try to refocus as to not get too caught up in this guy s backstory as it will probably never appear on TV.

I took a deep breath and open my mouth to sing. I was born for this.

 Sistah   You ve been on my mind

 Thank you, you can step back in line please.

That was it. That was as far as I had gotten in the audition before this jackass with a thinning mullet had cut me off.

Needless to say I did not go any further in the audition process. But then again I m guessing you knew that given the fact that this book is not touted as a tell-all from a previous *American Idol* contestant.

Look, I m not saying that *American Idol* ruined my dreams of becoming an international pop star, but they sure had a lot to do with it. That and I was *definitely* not the best undiscovered singer in America at that time. There s been so many of these talent shows that maybe I ve got a shot now. But I ve got a full-time job and a little more self-respect so maybe not.

The Exact Opposite of Judy Blume

I ve heard a lot of different things when I made it known that I was writing a book. Everything from Oh how exciting for you, to I didn t know you could read.

The most common things that I ve heard from people is that they wanted to know what kind of writer I was. Am I funny like Margaret Cho? Am I tackling serious topics like anyone from NPR? Do I write creepy shit like Stephen King? Is your book full of coming of age stories like Judy Blume?

I can tell you know that I am the exact opposite of Judy Blume. Judy Blume wrote the books that we all grew up with. She helped us through puberty, helped some of us with our first period, and she helped many of us deal with younger siblings so in many ways she an icon to several generations of people. I am none of those things.

Let s be honest here. I defy you to find any mention of anal sex in any of Judy Blume s books. That right there eliminates any comparison because let s face it the majority of this book is just one clever reference to anal after another.

I m almost one hundred percent positive that Judy Blume was never an Annie Lennox impersonating drag queen. I don t know her life like that, but I m pretty sure that s not something she puts on her resume and as far as I can tell it s not listed on her Wikipedia page.

Judy Blume is rolling in cash, I m still working a full-time job and self-publishing this dumpster fire of a book.

The list could go on for days about the ways that I am the opposite of what Judy Blume is as a writer, but I won t waste anymore of your time. I will leave you with some possible Judy Blume parody books I may write in the future:

Are You There God? He Went in Dry

Summer Fisters
Starring River S. Redd as Someone Who Has Their Shit Together

Actually, that last one s not too bad. I may keep that!

All I m actually saying is that if you re reading this book expecting
it to be some kind of literary revelation or the next great American
novel, I m sorry that you are going to be *sorely* disappointed in not
only your life choices, but mine as well.

Fucking Nerd!

I used to call myself a nerd, a geek, even a poindexter if I was feeling especially smart that day. I was into comic books, loved *Star Trek* and *Star Wars*, and I didn t really mind watching educational shit on TV. I still kind of consider myself a nerd. I still like all of those things plus a few more, but I m sexy about it. I only watch *Doctor Who* while I m plucking the hairs from my taint, I only read comic books in the nude, I make sure *Bill Nye the Science Guy* is playing in the background while I m having sex; you get the idea.

What I have learned though is that you cannot consider yourself a nerd after you visit any sort of fandom convention. I m not what you would consider an anime fan, I ll watch it if it s on, but I don t go out of my way to watch entire series, have a favorite *Dragon Ball* incarnation, and I didn t think the Netflix live-action *Deathnote* was all that bad.

A couple of years ago I went with some friends to the anime convention that is held here in the city I live in. We knew somebody who was participating in one of the panels and there was really nothing else happening that day.

Baby, when I tell you the people there were feeling the full and total fantasy would be the understatement of the year! Costumes and pageantry and production numbers galore! It was like some nerd version of the Emerald City. These people did not come to play!

Things took a dark and uncomfortable turn though. We go to the room that our friend s panel was taking place and this woman takes the stage. I guess she s leading the panel or whatever, I was never really clear on who she was. The topic of this panel was Idols.
So, I m thinking Ok cool, Japanese American Idol. I m totally here for this kind of shit! It was nothing like that at all.

In Japan, Idols are manufactured pop groups consisting of usually younger teenaged people who look super young and innocent. No big deal, right? Shouldn t have been, but then this woman goes on to talk about, in *great* detail, about this one idol that she s particularly fond of and how sexy they are. It was really gross because she was talking about a sixteen year old. SIXTEEN! Ma am this is a room full of people that you don t know and you are talking about how you want to fuck a sixteen year old. I was so uncomfortable.

After Pervy McPedophilepants got done talking, we learned that our friend and some other people would be recreating the opening to some super popular Idol anime openings. The other people in the audience went absolutely ape shit when the music started playing. They were up out of their seats and dancing; glow sticks came out of bags, there was one girl hula hooping. It was wild. I ve not seen this much excitement since I watched the One Direction concert DVD.

After the performance was over, we tried to go up to our friend to congratulate him on his performance, but he and the other performers were swarmed by the crowd wanting pictures and autographs. Insanity I tell you!

You think seeing pictures of Comicon will prepare you for actually experiencing a convention, it will not. There s a different vibe. It s a whole different world. It s like going to a sex club, there s a different electricity in the air than if you went to say the Home & Garden expo. Not to kink shame anyone, but I don t think Gary the House-Husband is getting off on pergolas the way nerds get off on anatomically correct Princess Leia statues. Do it though, go to a convention if for no other reason than to people watch. It s good to see other nerds in their natural habitat.

Also, don t mention that you liked the live-action *Deathnote*, you ll get killed.

Hi, I'm the Ugly Friend!

Not your dream date, but I'll do in a pinch!

It s not easy being the ugly friend. You re either funny or you re a cock block, there s no in between. Fortunately for me, I m funny I think.

Part of my struggle with mental illness is that I have incredibly low self-esteem. To counteract this I surround myself with very attractive people. All my friends are gorgeous And then there s me. I m small framed, crooked teeth, creepy smile, I always look tired, but god damn it I m hilarious I think.

I also feel like a bad gay sometimes because I have literally no ass. None. I m flatter than Sporty Spice back there. I thought maybe if I started wearing jockstraps instead of y know something that wasn t made of a maxi pad and two pieces of string I might get a little lift or something. That didn t happen and now I have a hundred dollars worth of jockstraps that I wear on the daily on principle alone.

I can hear you thinking: But, Greg, if you think you re so ugly doesn t surrounding yourself with beautiful people only make it worse for you? No, because not only am I your ugly, funny friend; I am also your ugly, funny, *easy* friend. It s easier to get into my pants than it is to get a reservation at a Red Roof Inn.

That was funnier in my head.

Also, I m the best wingman you ll ever have. I m witty enough to keep the object of your affections entertained while you bat your eyelashes and pay them all the compliments. I m a pro at this kind of shit. I tell the jokes while you play it cool, but I m never so funny as too draw all the attention away from you.

I ve always had body image issues, especially in a culture that says you re not attractive unless you ve got a six-pack, a perfect smile, and perfect hair. I have none of those things. Those issues only got worse when I got what is known as lipomas.

Lipomas are fatty deposits that build up under the skin. The usually occur on the upper torso and arms. I had one on my arm and one on my chin. The one on my chin got to be about the size of ping pong ball before I had finally had enough of looking like a monster. Armed with some iodine, aspercream, and a box cutter I got my mom to cut them out. I m an idiot, please don t do this. Go to the doctor like a normal person.

Sometimes we take drastic measures to look better. You can have your plastic surgery, having a family member cut things out of your face is metal as fuck   And pretty white trash, but whatever. I feel better about myself now that they re gone.

I ve done and tried just about everything to feel better about the way I look, short of having plastic surgery. That option isn t completely off the table   Yet.

I ve tried to have my hair cut in the same way as whatever celebrity is in right now. Let me just tell you that I *do not* look good with the Rachel.   I ve dyed my hair just about every color you can imagine. I ve gotten tattoos because I thought they would make me look edgy and cool. I still feel like the live action version of Doug Funnie.

I ve accepted that I m not traditionally good looking   Or non-traditionally good looking. Actually I don t know what either of those things mean I just know that I m not either. I m a right swipe on Tinder. That s a better way to describe it. I ve actually never been on Tinder so I don t know if that s correct or not.

When I was a kid I had what is now known as a hard luck case of gay face.   You know the look, almost cherub-like, clearly destined to enjoy the dick. Fortunately for me, as soon as the baby fat melted away, I was left with a chronic case of resting bitch face. I look constantly irritated. I mean, I am constantly irritated, but my face shows it more than others. I constantly hear: You should relax your face so you don t look so mean.   I ll let you in on a little secret: my face is perfectly relaxed; this is just how it looks.

Someone once asked why I refer to myself as the ugly friend and not the grenade? Because referring to someone, even myself, as a grenade is hateful. I might hate myself, but not enough to believe that flirting or even sleeping with me will destroy your reputation. I have other ways of doing that.

Victoria Beckham once said: I don t want to be seen eating or having fun.   This quote has always resonated with me. I hate the way I look when I smile, so if I don t smile when we re talking don t take it personal. I m not very photogenic anyway so chances are I ll make some stupid face or try to smize and look incredibly drunk thus making you look better. It works out for everyone.

I am incredibly drunk in this picture, but you get the point.

My self-deprecating humor is a defense mechanism. I know I m not cute, so I make all the jokes so you can t fuck up the punchlines.

Do Not Feed the Missionaries

Every gay guy I know has a fantasy about fucking a Mormon missionary. I am not exempt from this. Not sure what it is about them. Might be the conquest, might be the crisp shirts, might be the ties, could be the bikes, hell, it might even be an Osmond fetish-type thing. The point I m trying to make is that all gay men want to fuck a Mormon missionary.

You know what? It s that movie *Latter Days*. That s probably where it started. Probably.

I don t have the greatest track records when it comes to the type of missionaries that come and knock on your door. I was at home once and a couple of them came by. They fed me their song and dance about wanting to speak to me about saving my soul or whatever it is that they were into at that moment. I did all I could to try to shake them. Even my patented, I ll listen if we can all take our pants off and you don t mind if I touch myself while you talk didn t work.

So finally, I told them that if they took my garbage out, when they came back I would listen to everything they had to say. Surprisingly, they did it. When they came back I didn t answer the door, thus securing my place in hell.

Anyway, I asked a missionary that came into my store once if there was something that he wanted all the gays of the world to know. He said, and I quote, Please don t try to seduce us. Of course then I had to offer to suck his dick behind the dumpster.

Anatomy of a Hole Pic

I ve never quite figured out how to take a picture of my asshole. Weird, right? I m a gay man without a picture of his asshole on his phone.

I think the primary reason for this is because I m not *that* close with any of my friends. Surely, someone else has to be taking these pictures for y all. How do you even broach that topic with someone?

Hey, I m really trying to impress this person on **Insert Dating Site/Hookup App name here**, will you take a picture of my asshole?

Bro, help me take a new hole pic to send to them.

Is this how these conversations go? Do I need to step up my friend game? Or, like, is there that one friend that you have to take slutty pictures when you don t have a full length mirror or clean carpet?

If I m being honest, I did do a bit of research on the topic of hole pics. Firstly, *do not* use google because the FBI agent monitoring your internet usage is going to see some stuff you don t want to have to explain under threat of perjury.

I tried the whole over-the-shoulder mirror snap only to throw my back out and have to come up with a bullshit reason for walking funny the next day.

Then I tried the on the floor, ankles behind my ears picture only to find that it would be far easier to suck my own dick than get a decent picture of my anus. Plus side to this one is that I gained a new talent!

I was going to buy a selfie-stick and go that route, but I don t hate myself enough to own a selfie-stick or be seen in public purchasing one so that was definitely out.

Then I bit the bullet and asked a friend if they would do it for me. There s got to be some build up because you obviously can t just drop a bomb like that over pancakes at IHOP and expect to finish your meal with your friendship still intact.

I casually brought up hookup apps and how it was hard to take the perfect dick pic because while I think my dick looks amazing DonkeyPuncher945 says it s a little on the small side. The nerve of that guy!

I was quick to mention that I had never taken a hole pic because I wasn t quite smart enough to figure out how to make that work to which my friend responded by mentioning the ways I had already tried. This was already going downhill fast so I wasn t going to mention the fact that I had thrown my back out trying.

Surprisingly enough, apparently we are close enough that he offered to take one for me. In order to save face, I was like What? No Ok, sure.

The conclusion that I have made from this little experiment is:

1. I now have a hole pic phone-a-friend should the need ever come up.

2. No one s asshole is cute or attractive enough to warrant keeping a picture of it on your phone s camera roll. Not even your own.

It s for this reason that I don t keep my nudes on my phone. If you don t do that you don t ever have to worry about a friend seeing your dirty pictures or accidently sending Grandma a picture of your snatch when you re really trying to send a picture of the cupcakes you just made.

It s for this same reason that I don t trust keeping them on a cloud. People get hacked far too easily and far too often. I know I m not famous outside of my own mind, but all it s going to take is pissing off the right person and that one unflattering picture of you in a sexy Santa Claus thong from Frederick s of Hollywood that you sent to an ex-boyfriend is all over Facebook and Tumblr.

So Long, Farewell...

Hey! You made it to the end! Or maybe you didn t and this book is now sitting in your trashcan or on the back of your toilet for guests to read while they poop. Either way, congratulations! Unfortunately, your princess in another castle.

I had fun writing this book and I hope you ve enjoyed reading it. If you didn t, I can t promise I won t write another one because this was incredibly therapeutic and now that I ve done there might be more that I ve got to say. Truth be told, during the writing of this I ve already come up with one or two more ideas for future books. Whether or not that actually happens is a whole nother story.

I m sorry that there s not some big payoff here at the end. One more witty story to keep your attention. Chances are you ve knocked this out in the space of an afternoon. Maybe I ve photoshopped a dick in the background of one of the pictures that you can go try to find in a *Where's Wally?* twist that no one saw coming. Maybe I ve cleverly hidden a set of, possibly, winning lotter numbers throughout the pages that you can track down *Da Vinci Code* style. Is any of that true? Maybe, but you won t know until you give it a second look.

Perhaps you enjoyed this book enough to loan it to a friend or even your local library so it can be enjoyed by many generations to come. There is also the chance that you hated this book to the point that you ve thrown your entire e-reading device in the garbage then I hope the sanitation worker or homeless person that finds it can enjoy some of what I ve written.

Like I ve said before when I decided to write this book it wasn t to create the next great American novel and this *certainly* is not going to change people s lives. It might, it changed mine in that a lot of the thoughts and observations that were swirling around in my head are now down for other people to see. Maybe now the voices will be quiet and I can finally get a good night s sleep.

Acknowledgements
(In No Particular Order)

The Hugest of Thank You's to:

Annie Lennox and Jessica Lange, for without them I might have never had the drag career that I was gifted with.

My Atlanta family: Natalie, Mark, Ray, Laura, Seth, and a host of bartenders, servers, drag queens, and strippers for being some of the inspiration for this book.

Jenifer Lewis, Janet Hubert, and Gabrielle Union because I feel like we don't thank them enough.

My brothers, John and Ben, for putting up with me their entire lives.

My parents, obviously, for creating a legend.

Jessica Hall, whose excitement for this book really kept me going even when the inspiration was not there.

The most beautiful guy in all of Manchester! I love you!

To Any and every one that I've mentioned in this book, please don't sue me.

Made in the USA
Monee, IL
08 April 2021